Proactive Supplier Management in the Medical Device Industry

Also available from ASQ Quality Press:

Handbook of Investigation and Effective CAPA Systems, Second Edition
José Rodríguez-Pérez

How to Establish a Document Control System for Compliance with ISO 9001:2015, ISO 13485:2016, and FDA Requirements: A Comprehensive Guide to Designing a Process-Based Document Control System
Stephanie L. Skipper

Quality Risk Management in the FDA-Regulated Industry
José Rodríguez-Pérez

Statistical Process Control for the FDA-Regulated Industry
Manuel E. Peña-Rodríguez

The FDA and Worldwide Current Good Manufacturing Practices and Quality System Requirements Guidebook for Finished Pharmaceuticals
José Rodríguez-Pérez

A Practical Field Guide to ISO 13485
Erik V. Myhrberg and Joseph Raciti

The FDA and Worldwide Quality System Requirements Guidebook for Medical Devices, Second Edition
Amiram Daniel and Ed Kimmelman

Implementing ISO/IEC 17025:2005
Bhavan "Bob" Mehta

The Biomedical Quality Auditor Handbook, Second Edition
Biomedical Division and Bruce Haggar, editor

The Quality Toolbox, Second Edition
Nancy R. Tague

Root Cause Analysis: Simplified Tools and Techniques, Second Edition
Bjørn Andersen and Tom Fagerhaug

The ASQ Auditing Handbook, Fourth Edition
J.P. Russell, editor

To request a complimentary catalog of ASQ Quality Press publications, call 800-248-1946, or visit our website at http://www.asq.org/quality-press.

Proactive Supplier Management in the Medical Device Industry

James B. Shore and John A. Freije

ASQ Quality Press
Milwaukee, Wisconsin

American Society for Quality, Quality Press, Milwaukee 53203

Printed in the United States of America
21 20 19 18 17 16   5 4 3 2 1

Library of Congress Cataloging-in-Publication Data
Names: Shore, James B., 1965– author. | Freije, John A., 1964– author.
Title: Proactive supplier management in the medical device industry / James B. Shore and John A. Freije.
Description: Milwaukee, Wisconsin : ASQ Quality Press, [2016] | Includes bibliographical references and index.
Identifiers: LCCN 2016010120 | ISBN 9780873899314 (hardcover : alk. paper)
Subjects: LCSH: Medical instruments and apparatus industry—Management. | Production control.
Classification: LCC HD9994.A2 S56 2016 | DDC 681/.7610687—dc23
LC record available at https://lccn.loc.gov/2016010120

Publisher: Seiche Sanders
Acquisitions Editor: Matt Meinholz
Managing Editor: Paul Daniel O'Mara
Production Administrator: Randall Benson

Printed on acid-free paper

Quality Press
600 N. Plankinton Ave.
Milwaukee, WI 53203-2914
E-mail: authors@asq.org
ASQ **The Global Voice of Quality**®

Table of Contents

List of Figures and Tables

CD Contents

FDA Industry-Basics, Purchasing Controls, November 4, 2015, presentation

FDA Preamble to 21 CFR 820

GHTF/SG3/N17:2008 Quality Management System—Medical Devices—Guidance on the Control of Products and Services Obtained from Suppliers

NBOG BPG 2010-1 Guidance for Notified Bodies auditing suppliers to medical device manufacturers

Supplier Controls: FDA Perspective, MEDCON 2012 presentation

Example Supplier Quality Agreement

FDA Compliance Program Guidance Manual, Program 7382.845, Inspection of Medical Device Manufacturers

Self-Assessment Tool

Supplier Selection Road Map

Total Risk Factor (TRF) Tool

Example Supplier Survey

Quality Audit Information

Example Quality Audit Checklist

Audit Cover Sheet

Supplier Evaluation Summary

Example Supplier Change Notification Form

Example Sterilization Verbiage and Process Control Form

Foreword

Purchasing controls and supplier management continue to be target-rich environments resulting in investigators from the Food and Drug Administration (FDA) issuing a mountain of Form 483 observations, some of which lead to an eventual warning letter from the agency. The medical device industry continues to struggle with the implementation of both adequate procedures and effective tools needed to manage suppliers. Compliance with 21 CFR, Part 820.50, is the goal; however, the requirements are fairly interpretive, which allows the device establishments some proverbial wiggle room to achieve compliance. Interpretive regulations will result in compliance issues. Authors Jim Shore and John Freije are dedicated industry professionals who provide the readers of their book with a plethora of practical information and tools that can be readily applied to any quality management system. Their approach for managing suppliers has been industry tested and proven to be appropriate, effective, and scalable for device establishments of all sizes. In fact, I consider this book a must-read for all industry professionals. Readers will benefit from the life experiences and supplier management tools compiled and presented in this one book.

Dr. Christopher J. Devine
President, Devine Guidance International

Preface

We would like to thank you for reading our book, *Proactive Supplier Management in the Medical Device Industry*. Whether you purchased this book or it was given to you as a gift, we truly appreciate your taking the time to read it, and we hope that you'll apply the concepts that we've developed from our years of experience of working with suppliers.

We also hope that you enjoy this aspect of the quality system regulation as much as we do. When we set out to write this book, we wanted to make sure that you could immediately apply what we have put together in this book. We provide best practices based on a combined 50+ years of quality and engineering experience, working with some of the best medical device companies and contract manufacturers in the world. The approach we took in writing this book was not just to quote the Quality System Regulation or ISO standard, but to also have you apply some of the tools that we mention throughout the book so that you may have a compliant, robust, and flexible system.

Jim was once asked, "What would motivate anyone to write a book and share all their great ideas?" The answer is simple—we work in the best industry in the world, and we improve the lives of patients all over the world. Today, there are few people who can say the medical device industry hasn't touched someone close to them, their family, or even themselves. Had it not been for the modern technology that was available, Jim's daughter would not have survived the cardiac disease that was found during the second trimester of his wife's pregnancy.

The quality of devices used every day relies on the best supplier management tools. With this flexibility, these tools can be used for all types of suppliers as well as be applicable to combination devices based on the risk profile.

If you recall from the preamble to the 1996 Quality System Regulation, comment #106, the intent of purchasing controls is as follows:

> The intent of Sec. 820.50 is to ensure that device manufacturers select only those suppliers, contractors, and consultants who have the capability to provide quality product and services. As with finished devices, quality cannot be inspected or tested into products or services.

That being said, the intent of this book is to show you a process of effectively selecting, evaluating, and implementing applicable controls based on the evaluation and ongoing proactive management of suppliers, consultants, and contractors in a state of compliance. These processes can be applied to all suppliers, contractors, and consultants. However, the difference will lie with the risk associated with the product or service obtained.

You should know that with your purchase of this book you are supporting the troops, as the authors' profits from book sales will be donated to veteran organizations. Both authors are veterans of this great country and felt this would be a great way to pay it forward.

"If you can read this, thank a teacher. If you like your freedom, thank a veteran."

#payitforward

#freedomisntfree

ACKNOWLEDGMENTS

Special thanks to those people who contributed to the book:

- Steven Walfish, for providing us technical support on the inspection portion regarding statistics
- Bill Alrich, for providing us technical support and feedback throughout the book and for always having a great sense of humor
- Barry Craner, who also provided us with great feedback on our book, and for his support as a great mentor within the medical device community

Jim would also like to thank:

- Stephen Perez, a great boss and mentor, who taught me the importance of prioritization that applies not only to work but to my life as well
- Peter Ashe, another great boss and mentor, for allowing me to implement critical-to-quality characteristics into the engineering documentation and start the supplier control plans
- Steve McKenna, for allowing me to implement supplier controls at an enterprise level and for sharing the same passion for putting in the right controls and not accepting the "one size fits all" approach
- Lesley, my wife, for allowing me to take time away from the family to work on the book and for being my biggest supporter
- My partner in crime, John, who has pushed me when I needed it and whose great ideas have made this book even better

John would also like to thank:

- Kristin, my wife, for picking up the slack when I spent numerous hours working on the book with Jim and for being my number one supporter
- Carl and Beverly Freije, my parents, who provided me with the tools to succeed in life. I wish they were around to read this book—may they rest in peace
- My good friend and colleague Jim Shore, who can always give me a good laugh and whose great ideas also made this a great book

Road Map to Supplier Quality Management

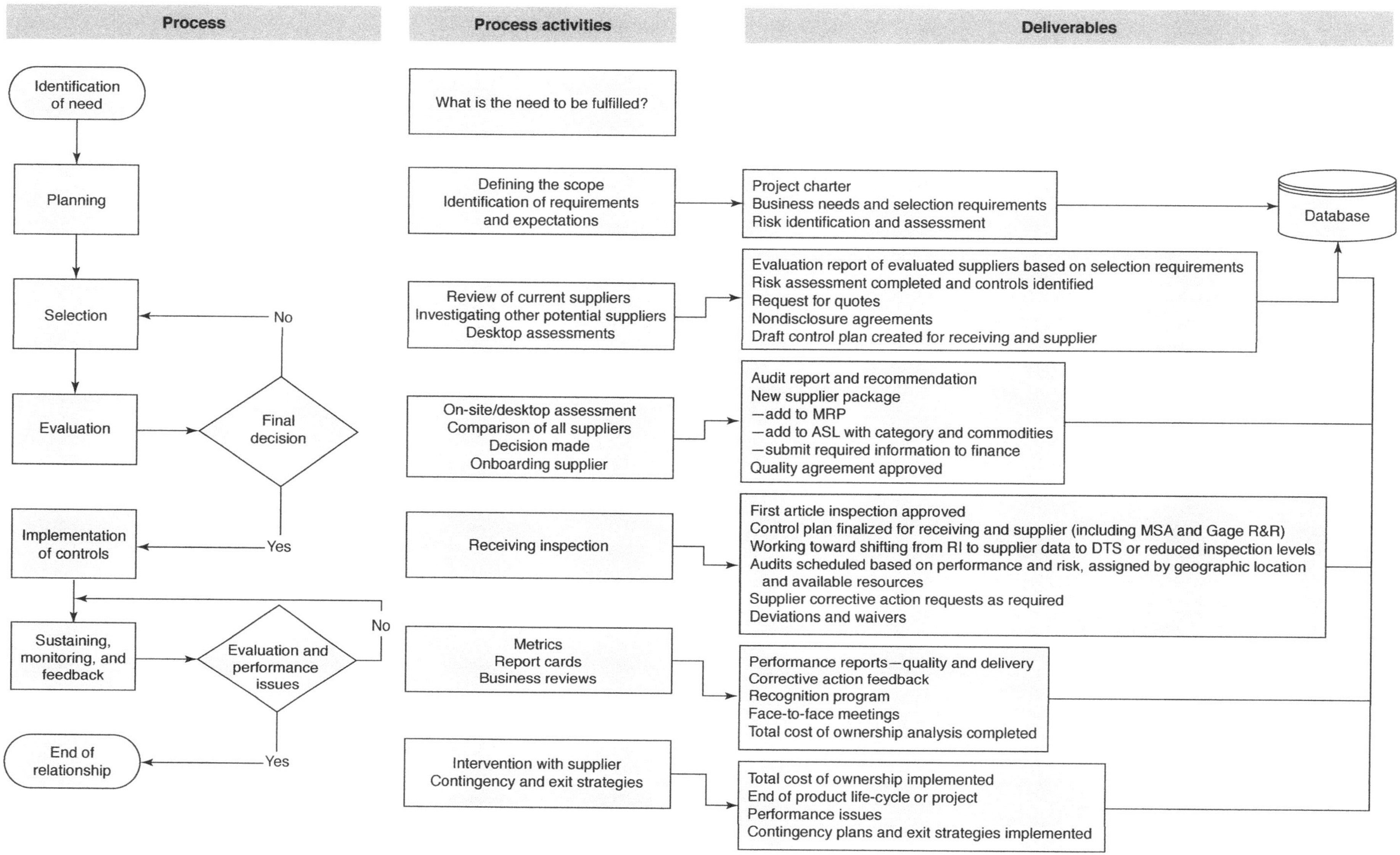

1

Introduction: Why Do We Need to Do This?

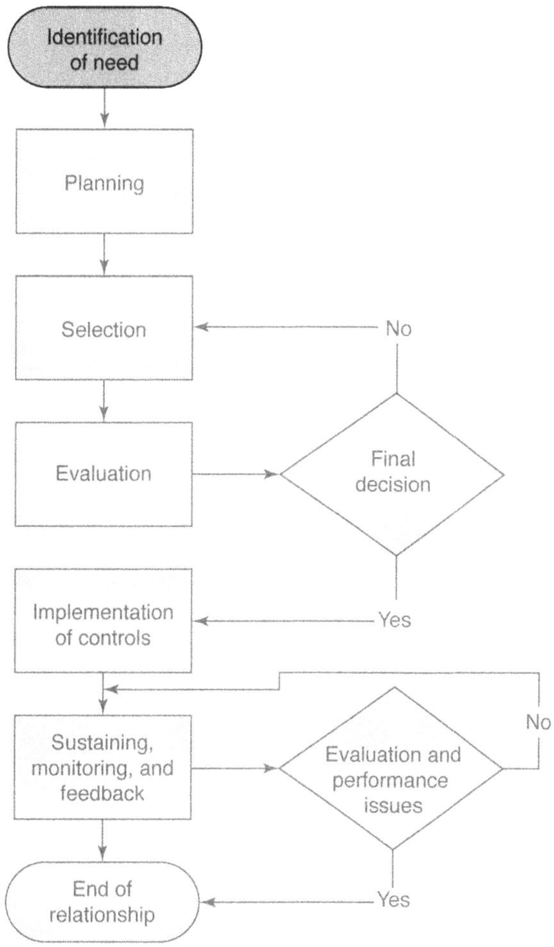

In *Juran's Quality Handbook*, author Joseph Juran speaks to a strategic view with supplier relationships as opposed to the traditional view (what we call the old "whip and chain"). Some of the items he points out, to name a few, are how the relationship in the traditional view is more short-term adversarial versus the longer-term partnership in the strategic view, how we don't trust the supplier, and how we are focused only on the price and not on the total cost of ownership (Juran and Godfrey 1999, p. 21.6). Having a strategic view with your suppliers can make for a better relationship for all parties involved, with the main focus being the safety of the end user.

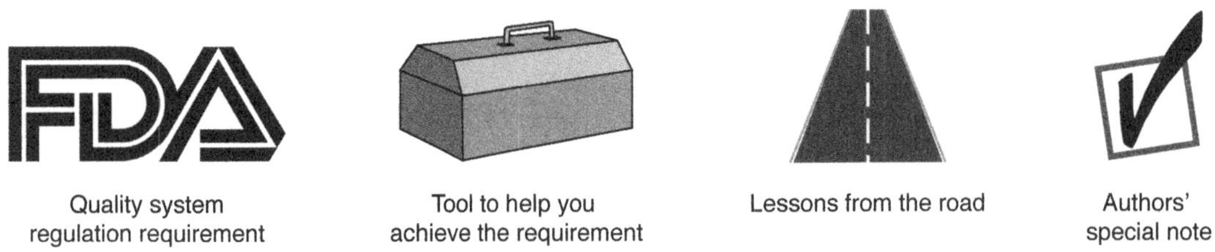

Figure 1.1 Icons used in this book.

The examples and models found in this book are ones that either we ourselves have implemented or other great companies have implemented. Our philosophy is "Plagiarism is the best form of flattery, but poor implementation of a good idea is just plain bad."

First, always acknowledge the person/company whose concept you saw—that's just good professional behavior. Second, if you find that your results are the same as those of the original founder, then document what went well and use that baseline for making further improvements. Third, for the tools and concepts found in this book, use them to make improvements within your own quality system. If you have issues, please send an e-mail or call us so we can help you.

The FDA and toolbox icons in Figure 1.1 will assist you throughout the book in determining whether it's a requirement or a tool to help you achieve compliance. In "Lessons from the road" we share our real-life stories and what we have learned throughout our careers. We'll keep the stories short, but we promise there's something to be learned from them. The check mark is used to highlight key thoughts or what we feel are takeaways or a special focus.

INTRODUCTION TO THE FDA, ISO, GHTF, AND NBOG

You might be asking, why is it important that I care about my supplier's processes? Besides the regulatory requirement to evaluate, select, and control your suppliers, there is an old saying that "junk in = junk out." In order for you to have high confidence in the reliability of your devices, you must ensure each and every component or service meets your requirements, including quality requirements. So you should look at it as not only a regulatory requirement but also a business aspect. Poorly functioning devices can lead to:

- Death or serious injury to the patient (you or someone close to you) or the healthcare provider
- Customer dissatisfaction or departure to your competitor's device
- Recall or market withdrawal of your product
- Your company's reputation being ruined
- Jail time or being disbarred from working in the industry

Following is a brief introduction to the Food and Drug Administration's (FDA's) regulation and the International Organization for Standardization's (ISO's) standard on the assessment of purchasing controls for medical device companies. After that is a brief overview of the Global Harmonization Task Force (GHTF) and Notified Body Operations Group (NBOG) guidance documents used to help establish an effective and compliant purchasing controls process for medical device manufacturers. The history of the FDA and those of the other regulatory bodies will not be discussed.

We promise to keep it brief, as it's not the primary focus of the book, but it is important to know these key facts. You may want to return to these sections later in the book, as they will be helpful when you create or review your current supplier quality methodology.

Please note that some people will skip this section altogether, but we recommend that you at least skim through it. As with the preamble to 21 CFR (Code of Federal Regulations) 820, there is a great deal of good information found in the beginning of any document.

This chapter contains a high-level overview of the FDA's Quality System Regulation 21 CFR 820.50, ISO's 13485:2016 subclause 7.4, GHTF's guidance document SG3/N17/2008, *Quality Management System—Medical Devices—Guidance on the Control of Products and Services Obtained from Suppliers*, and NBOG's BPG 2010-1—*Guidance for Notified Bodies auditing suppliers to medical device manufacturers.*

For those of you who are new to the medical device industry, the ISO is the world's largest developer and publisher of International Standards. The FDA is responsible for protecting the health of the public by ensuring the safety, efficacy, and security of human and veterinary drugs, biological products, medical devices, our nation's food supply, cosmetics, and products that emit radiation. To learn more about the ISO and the FDA, you can visit them at http://www.iso.org and http://www.fda.gov, respectively.

Although officially decommissioned, the GHTF documents are still highly referred to and used. The purpose of the GHTF was to encourage convergence in regulatory practices related to ensuring the safety, effectiveness, performance, and quality of medical devices; promote technological innovation; and facilitate international trade. The primary way in which this purpose was accomplished was through the publication and dissemination of harmonized documents on basic regulatory practices. These documents were developed by five GHTF study groups and provided a model for the regulation of medical devices that could then be adopted and implemented by national regulatory authorities. Unlike regulations and standards, guidance documents are not legally enforced but are widely used by regulatory bodies as the industry guidelines and generally thought of as the current thinking. The best benefit of guidance documents is that they are free and can be reproduced and copied with no restrictions.

With the decommissioning of the GHTF in 2012, all the documents can be found under the newly formed International Medical Device Regulators Forum (IMDRF) (http://www.imdrf.org; from the home page, follow the link to the GHTF archive).

The final organization that will be touched on is the NBOG. The purpose of the NBOG is to improve the overall performance of notified bodies in the medical device sector by primarily identifying and promulgating examples of best practices to be adopted by both notified bodies and those organizations responsible for their designation and control. To learn more about the NBOG, go to http://www.nbog.eu.

TERMS AND DEFINITIONS

The following terms and definitions are not all-inclusive but are common in the purchasing controls process. Definitions taken from 21 CFR 820.3, 21 CFR 807.20(a)(1)(2), and GHTF Guidance SG4/N33R16 are copied in their entirety, while terms from ISO 9000:2005 are paraphrased in the authors' words.

Specification Developer (21 CFR 807.20(a)(1))

Develops specifications for a device that is distributed under the establishment's own name but performs no manufacturing. This includes establishments that, in addition to developing specifications, also arrange for the manufacturing of devices labeled with another establishment's name by a contract manufacturer (http://www.fda.gov/MedicalDevices/DeviceRegulationandGuidance/HowtoMarketYourDevice/RegistrationandListing/ucm053165.htm#specification).

Manufacturer (21 CFR 820.3(o))

Means any person who designs, manufactures, fabricates, assembles, or processes a finished device. Manufacturer includes but is not limited to those who perform the functions of contract sterilization, installation, relabeling, remanufacturing, repacking, or specification development, and initial distributors of foreign entities performing these functions.

It should be noted that the Manufacturer can outsource goods and services but not regulatory responsibility or product liability. The manufacturer's name listed on the device has the ultimate responsibility for the device.

Component (21 CFR 820.3(c))

Means any raw material, substance, piece, part, software, firmware, labeling, or assembly which is intended to be included as part of the finished, packaged, and labeled device.

Manufacturing Material (21 CFR 820.3(p))

Means any material or substance used in or used to facilitate the manufacturing process, a concomitant constituent, or a byproduct constituent produced during the manufacturing process, which is present in or on the finished device as a residue or impurity not by design or intent of the manufacturer.

Establish (21 CFR 820.3(k))

Means to define, document (in writing or electronically), and implement.

Supplier (ISO 9000:2005)

Entity that provides a product (could be an organization or individual; Internal or external to the organization).

Service (Comment #102, Preamble to the 1996 Quality System Regulation)

Means parts of the manufacturing or quality system that are contracted to others, for example, plating of metals, testing, and sterilizing, among others.

Critical Supplier (GHTF SG4/N33R16)

Supplier delivering materials, components, or services that may influence the safety and performance of the product.

We would like to add that this definition is somewhat broad, as pretty much any component that does not meet the manufacturer's specifications has the potential to affect the safety and performance of the product. As discussed in later chapters, the use of risk assessment to determine the severity of the components' risk to the finished medical device must be conducted. Using a tool such as failure modes and effects analysis (FMEA) is recommended for assessing the risk of your components, which will in turn be used to drive your supplier's rating.

Process (ISO 9000:2005)

Activities (interrelated or interacting) that transform inputs into outputs.

Product (21 CFR 820.3(r))

Means components, manufacturing materials, in-process devices, finished devices, and returned devices.

Product (ISO 9000:2005)

Results of a process; contains four generic categories: hardware, software, processed material, and services.

INTENT OF PURCHASING CONTROLS

Figure 1.2 visually communicates the continual cycle of the purchasing controls process to ensure safe and effective devices are distributed for use. This verbiage is extracted from comment #99 of the FDA's preamble to the 1996 Quality System Regulation (QSReg).

FDA AND ISO REGULATIONS PERTAINING TO PURCHASING CONTROLS AND THEIR DIFFERENCES

Table 1.1 displays both the FDA's regulation and the two ISO standards used by medical device suppliers and accepted by a large portion of medical device companies.

Most medical device companies will give preference to ISO 13485 as it is industry specific, but it is not required unless you are a finished device manufacturer distributing

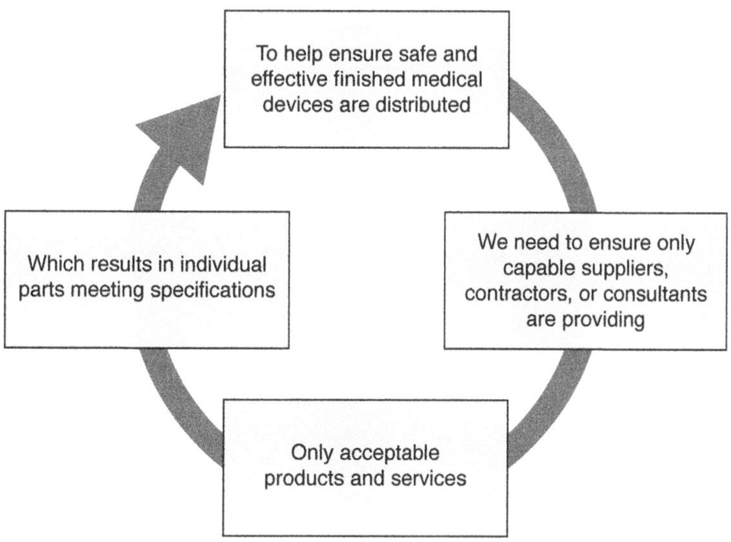

Figure 1.2 Intent of purchasing controls.

Table 1.1 Overview of ISO standards and FDA regulation.

ISO 13485:2016	Medical devices—Quality management systems—Requirements for regulatory purposes	European standard on quality management systems that applies specifically to medical device manufacturers
ISO 9001:2015	Quality management systems—requirements	European standard on quality management systems that is not industry specific
FDA 21 CFR 820 FDA	Quality system regulation	US regulation governing finished device manufacturers

medical devices in the European Union (EU) or your customer mandates it through a contract. ISO 13485 is industry specific to medical devices, whereas 9001 is applicable to anyone providing a product or service. As stated under 21 CFR 820.1(a)(1) Applicability, "Quality System Regulation does not apply to manufacturers of components or parts of finished devices, but the FDA does highly encourage those types of manufacturers to follow the regulation as guidance" (preamble comment #99, p. 52624). In ISO 13485:2016, verbiage has been added under subclause 0.1 General about suppliers voluntarily following this standard when providing product to a medical device company.

However, medical device manufacturers *do not have an option* for compliance with 21 CFR 820 if they manufacture, import, or offer for import in any state or territory of the United States, the District of Columbia, or the Commonwealth of Puerto Rico.

Table 1.2 displays a high-level summary of the slight differences between the two ISO standards and the Quality System Regulation (QSReg). The book will use QSReg as the abbreviation for Quality System Regulation since the use of QSR is defined as a Quality System Record per 21 CFR 820.186.

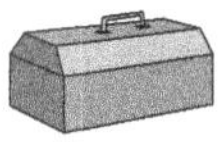

Table 1.2 provides a comparison of 21 CFR 820, ISO 13485, and ISO 9001 specific to purchasing controls.

Table 1.2 Overview of ISO standard and FDA regulation similarities and differences.

Regulation/standard	Similarities	Differences
820.50(a)(1)(2)(3) Purchasing controls 13485 7.4.1 Purchasing process 9001:2015 8.4.1, 8.4.2 Purchasing process (General and Type and extent of control) *Includes the selection, evaluation, type and extent of controls, and documentation*	For the most part, the intents of all three are similar, but 13485 and 820 require the manufacturer to develop and maintain procedures for purchasing controls	9001:2015 Purchasing requirements moved to subclause 8.4, which is under the heading of "Operations" Still no procedural requirement called out
820.50(b) Purchasing data 13485 7.4.2 Purchasing information 9001:2015 8.4.3 Information for external providers *Includes clear and concise quality and product requirements*	The intents of the regulation and standards are similar	The regulation contains a requirement to obtain an agreement, where possible, with the supplier to notify the manufacturer of any changes. ISO 13485:2003 does not contain such a requirement, but ISO 13485:2016 does. ISO 9001:2015 does not.
820.80(b) Receiving acceptance activities 13485 7.4.3 Verification of purchased product 9001:2015 8.6 Release of products and services *Includes verification of your purchased products generally through incoming inspection activities*	The intents of the regulation and standards are similar	The standards contain a scenario where the organization may seek to verify purchased product at the supplier's location. ISO 9001:2015 does not explicitly state it that way, but the intent may be implied based on the verbiage used about planned arrangements with the customer being met. Verification of purchased product is not contained within the purchasing subclause in the regulation, as it has its own subclause 21 CFR 820.80. ISO 9001:2015 has moved this to subclause 8.6 with a title of "Release of products and services."

Since we did not want to inundate you with a chapter full of regulations, each section of 21 CFR 820.50 and 820.80(b) as well as ISO 13485 subclause 7.4 will be covered in later chapters so the point can be emphasized with regard to compliance of the regulation subclause. Since there are copyrights protecting ISO standards, ISO requirements will only be paraphrased. Any forms provided with specific regulatory requirements will use FDA regulations, as they are not mandated by copyright laws. When citing FDA regulations or guidance documents, we will do our best to ensure the FDA source is referenced. For alignment with ISO 13485 subclause 7.4.3, Verification of purchased product, we consider part 820.80(b) *Receiving acceptance activities* as part of the purchasing controls process. "There is a very direct relationship between purchasing controls and acceptance activities," says Kim Trautman (quoted in Schmitt 2008, p. 1), former associate director for international affairs, Office of the Center Director, and FDA's Medical Device International Quality Systems Expert. "As our industry has been stretched globally, we have seen many more problems in both of these areas." Therefore, the content of this book includes both elements to ensure the most robust process to address purchasing controls concerns.

NBOG EXPECTATIONS

In March 2010 the NBOG issued NBOG 2010-1—*Guidance for Notified Bodies auditing suppliers to medical device manufacturers*. This document gives guidance to notified bodies on auditing the purchasing controls process of medical device manufacturers. The guidance considers the purchasing controls process to be a critical aspect for those manufacturers that outsource critical processes—for example, sterilization, design and development, contract manufacturing, or other services where full verification may not be possible. The main objective of the guidance is to ensure outsourced processes, whether for a service or product, provided by suppliers comply with the manufacturer's requirements. The guidance has five major steps that will be discussed later in the book but are listed here:

1.1 Verify that procedures for conducting supplier evaluations have been established. (ISO 13485:2003: 7.4.1)

1.2 Verify that the manufacturer evaluates and maintains effective controls over suppliers, so that specified requirements are met. (ISO 13485:2003: 7.4.1)

1.3 Verify that the manufacturer assures the adequacy of specifications for products and services that suppliers are to provide, and defines risk management responsibilities and any necessary risk control measures. (ISO 13485:2003: 7.4.2)

1.4 Verify that records of supplier evaluations are maintained. (ISO 13485:2003: 7.4.1)

1.5 Determine that the verification of purchased products and services is adequate. (ISO 13485:2003: 7.4.3)

Though this document may not directly apply to your company, it can be a great resource to help define critical suppliers to your company along with the use of the risk management tools. Since publication of the NBOG in 2010, ISO 13485:2003 has been updated to ISO 13485:2016, but the principles are still the same.

GHTF SG3 DOCUMENT AND FLOWCHART

As previously stated, the GHTF has been decommissioned, but some of the work it accomplished has been transferred to the IMDRF website and is still accessible. The IMDRF will build on the strong foundational work the GHTF started, and the GHTF documents are still widely used as guidance documents for the industry.

In December 2008 GHTF Study Group 3 released GHTF/SG3/N17:2008—*Quality Management System—Medical Devices—Guidance on the Control of Products and Services Obtained from Suppliers*. As the name implies, the document provides guidance to medical device manufacturers on the control of products and services obtained from suppliers. This is mentioned on slide 13 of the FDA's "Purchasing Controls" webinar, which is included on the CD accompanying this book. Recall from the ISO definition of product paraphrased earlier that product consists of four generic categories of hardware, software, processed materials, and services.

The guidance document has been broken into six phases for the establishment of controls of products and services obtained from suppliers. The six phases are as follows:

1. Planning
2. Selection of potential supplier(s)
3. Supplier evaluation and acceptance
4. Finalization of controls
5. Delivery, measurement, and monitoring
6. Feedback and communication, including corrective action and preventive action process

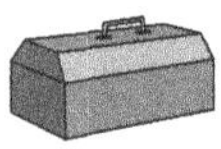

The flow of the book follows an approach similar to this guidance. From our experience we felt this was a robust model to assimilate. Each phase will be described later in the book in the applicable chapter.

We also believe that since purchasing requirements for both ISO 13485 and the FDA are very similar in nature, regardless of what country you are in, following the tools provided and using the best practices taken from the GHTF guidance on supplier controls can greatly reduce your chance of being noncompliant. See Figure 1.3 for an overview of the GHTF six-step process.

OVERVIEW OF FDA ENFORCEMENT TRENDS SPECIFIC TO SUPPLIER CONTROLS

Figures 1.4 and 1.5 provide an overview of the total number of warning letters spanning from 2004 to 2014 and the percentage of those letters that contained observations for purchasing controls.

When analyzing the graph in Figure 1.4, it almost appears to be cyclical in nature, where warning letters containing purchasing controls observations appear to increase every three years and then drop off. Since data are missing for 2003, this observation is based on the data from 2006 to 2012, but one cannot ignore the slight increase from 2004 to 2005 and then the drop-off in 2006.

Further analysis of Figure 1.4 shows that on average roughly 40% of the warning letters issued during this time frame contained observations for purchasing controls (reference the running average line). Even though there is a slight decline from its peak in 2005, the running average has been holding at about 40% since 2006, and there is a steady increase in both the number of warning letters issued and the number of warning letters containing cites against purchasing controls. Figure 1.5 contains the analysis of the individual QSReg cited.

Since tracking the warning letters from 2004 QSReg 820.80(b), "receiving acceptance activities" has been the number-one-cited observation related to purchasing controls, as displayed by the Pareto analysis in Figure 1.5. The second-most-cited observation is QSReg 820.50(a)(1) "evaluation and selection"; combining these two observations accounts for approximately 45% of all purchase control observations. We believe that if you follow the guidance in this book, your chances of getting a warning letter are greatly reduced, as this book is based on the most current guidance with regard to purchasing controls. As stated in the preface, we teach you a process of effectively selecting, evaluating, and implementing applicable controls based on the evaluation and ongoing management of your purchasing controls process in a state of compliance.

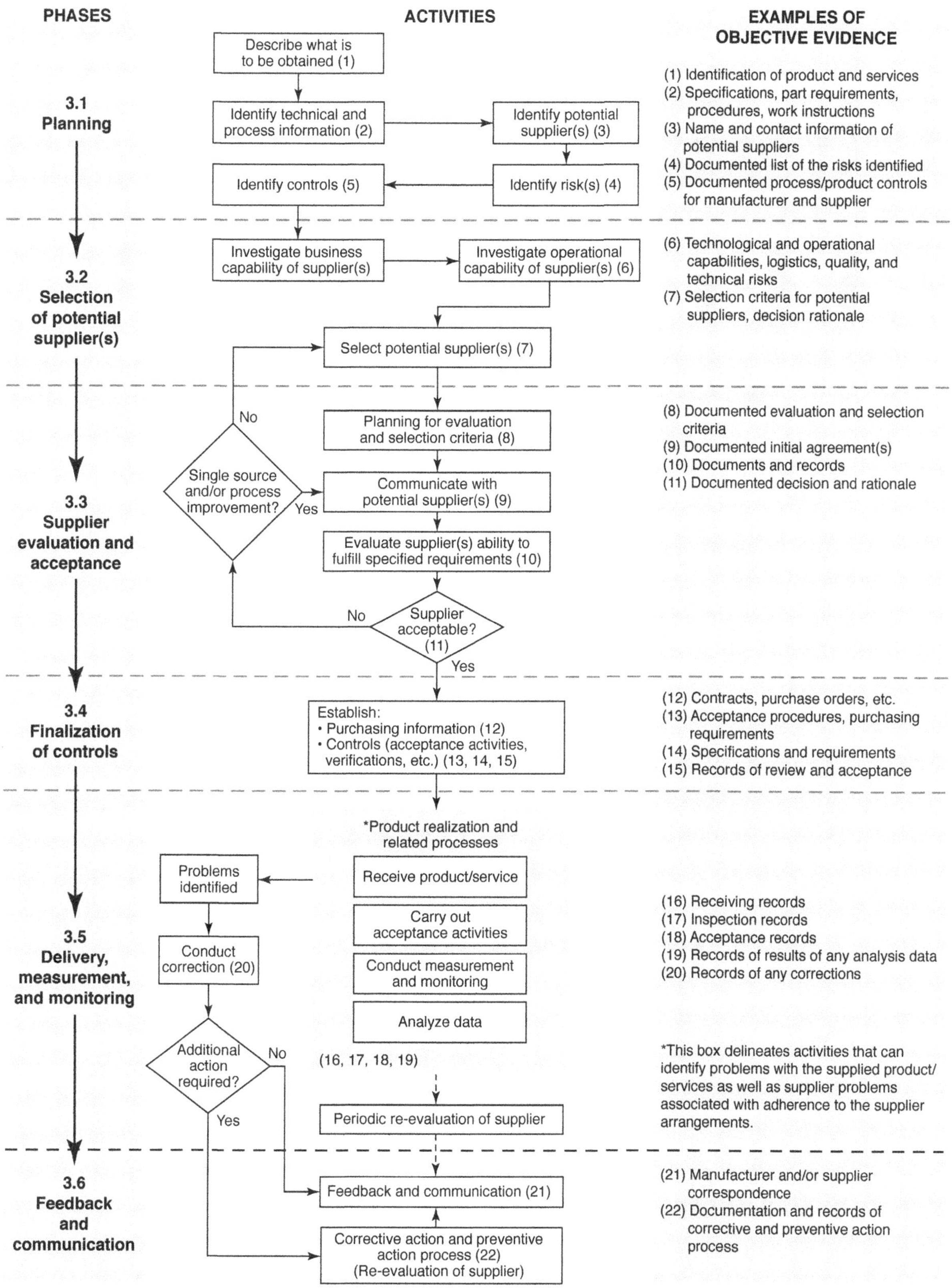

Figure 1.3 GHTF phase overview for supplier controls.

Note: The depicted activities in this figure are not meant to be strictly sequential. In certain cases they may occur in parallel.

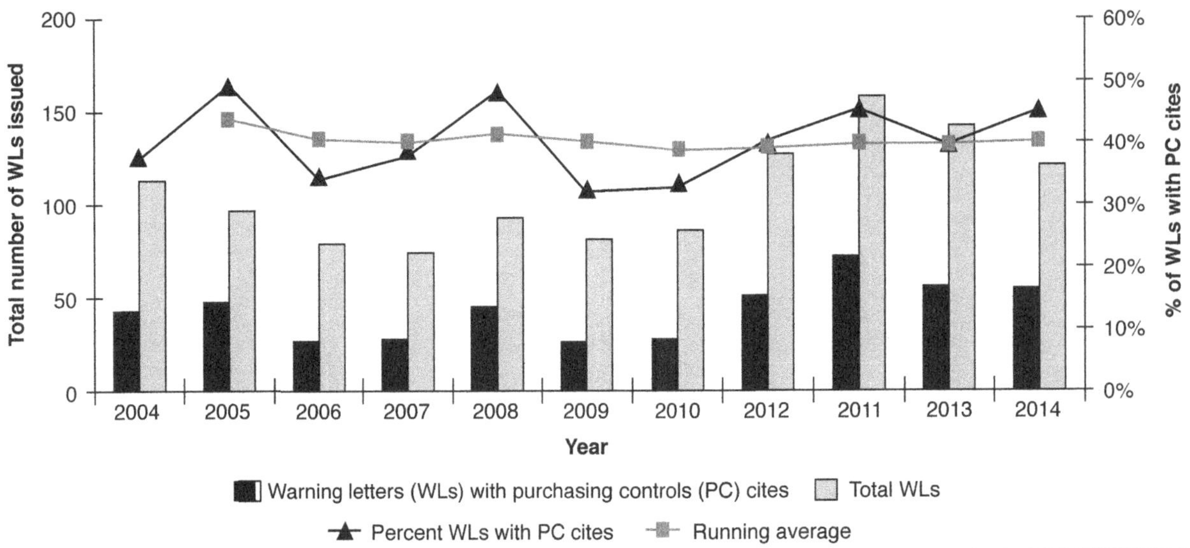

Figure 1.4 Warning letters with purchasing controls cites (2004–2014).

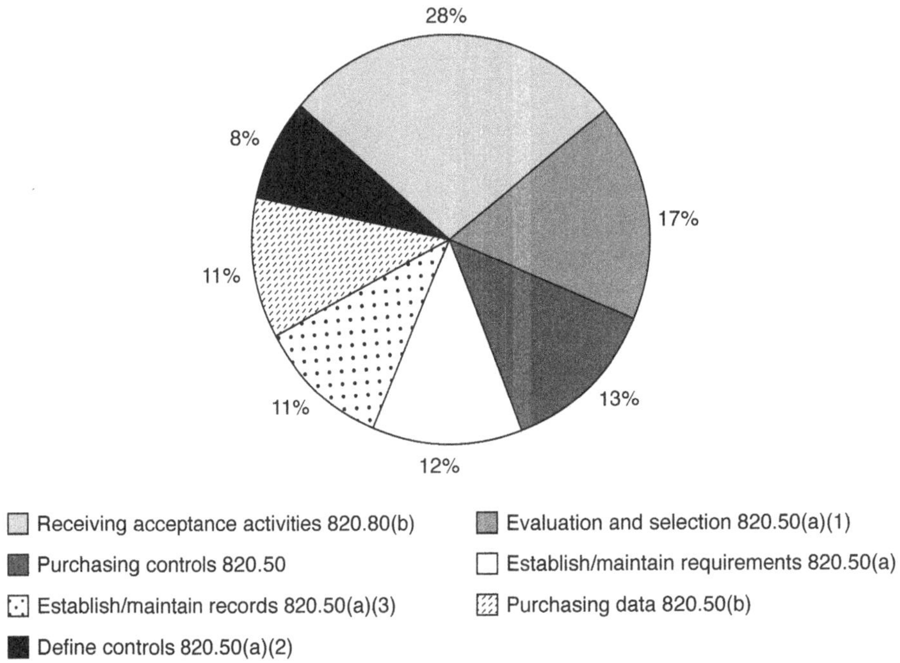

Figure 1.5 Breakdown of purchasing controls cites (2004–2014).

IMPORTANCE OF ESTABLISHING AN EFFECTIVE PURCHASING CONTROLS PROCESS

From the data provided in Figures 1.4 and 1.5, one can see that the primary reason for establishing an effective purchasing controls process is to reduce the potential of a warning letter being issued to your company, but the bottom line is that it's the regulation. By "effective," we mean that the purchasing process is compliant with the regulation and standards and not bypassed because it is overly complicated, and that it is not too lenient that suppliers with poor quality management systems are accepted without stringent controls.

However, we believe that in addition to meeting the compliance aspect of the regulation and standards, there are other reasons to establish an effective purchasing controls process:

- Reduces the risk of being noncompliant with regulatory bodies
- Reduces the potential of receiving nonconforming product
- Lets you determine and monitor the controls that are needed at your supplier based on risk involved, specifically:
  - Links the specific requirements of 21 CFR 820.70(a)(2)
  - Monitoring and control of process parameters and component and device characteristics during production
- Provides consolidation of the supplier base when necessary
- Avoids relying on companies with limited or no knowledge of medical risk factors and regulatory requirements
- Makes good business sense
- And most important, helps prevent a serious injury or death to the patient (you or someone close to you) or the healthcare provider (Figure 1.6)

The following excerpts from warning letters say something different. We've outlined only an excerpt of each letter to avoid pointing out any single company, and the examples presented represent each area of the purchasing controls process. To emphasize the purchasing controls process, additional examples from warning letters will be presented in subsequent chapters.

Example 1 is related to the lack of any process whatsoever for purchasing controls. For an inspector, it does not get any easier than having the individual tell you they don't have a process in place.

> Failure to establish procedures to ensure that all purchased or otherwise received product and services conform to specified requirements, as required by 21 CFR 820.50.

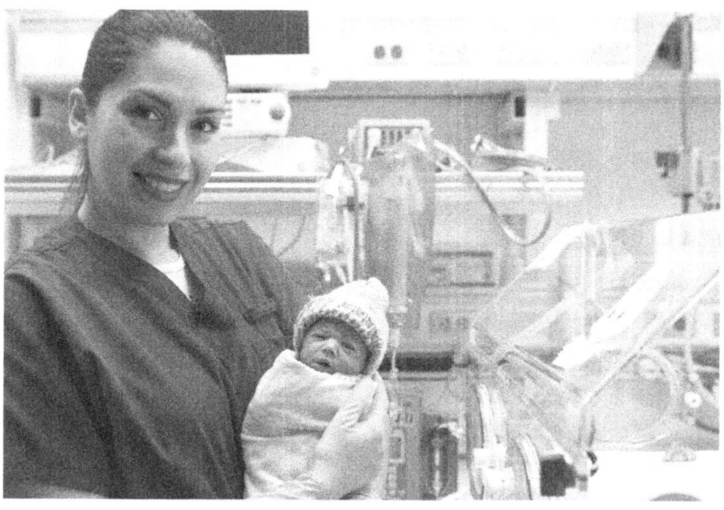

Figure 1.6 Nurse with a newborn and several devices.
Source: Thinkstock.

For example, when asked by the investigator, staff at your firm replied that your firm has no purchasing control procedures and no procedures to address the evaluation of suppliers and describe specified quality requirements for components.

Example 2 is related to the lack of adequate requirements that must be met by suppliers.

Failure to establish and maintain the requirements, including the quality requirements that must be met by suppliers, contractors, and consultants. 21 C.F.R. 820.50(a). For example, your procedure for Purchasing, SOP 06-01, Rev. 3 and Vendor Survey, Form No. 06-01-04, Rev. 1 are inadequate in that they do not require an evaluation and qualification determination of vendors, suppliers, and contract service providers listed on your firm's Approved Vendors List prior to February 28, 2003. There is no documentation that (b)(4)., the supplier of extruded titanium tubes used in the manufacture of Brachytherapy seeds, was qualified or requalified as a supplier. Your firm has been purchasing extruded titanium tubes from this vendor since prior to 2003.

Example 3 is related to the lack of adequate evaluation of suppliers. In Chapter 3 we discuss adding requirements to your supplier survey that must be met by your suppliers.

Failure to evaluate and select suppliers, contractors, and consultants based on their ability to meet specified requirements, which is required by 21 CFR 820.50(a)(1). Specifically, there is no documented evidence of suppliers, contractors, or consultants being evaluated and selected based on their ability to meet specified requirements, including quality requirements. The procedure "Supplier Qualification and Approval," QP74-001, Revision 1, step (b)(4) states "Suppliers shall be evaluated on the basis of their ability to meet specified requirements."

Example 4 is related to the lack of adequate controls based on the extent of evaluation. Chapter 4 discusses applicable controls based on the evaluation.

Failure to define the type and extent of control to be exercised over the product, services, suppliers, contractors, and consultants, based on the evaluation results, as required by 21 CFR 820.50(a)(2). Specifically, your procedure entitled "Purchasing" (SOP010, Rev. (b)(4)) fails to provide a process defining the type and extent of control to be exercised over component suppliers requiring a second review due to the supplier being classified "(b)(4)."

Example 5 is related to the lack of adequate records being established and maintained. Chapter 4 discusses pertinent records that need to be maintained.

a. There is no documentation that the (b)(4) was evaluated and qualified to conduct equipment calibration.

b. There is no documentation that the quality consultant, (b)(4), was evaluated and qualified by the firm.

c. There is no documentation that (b)(4) was evaluated and qualified to perform this service.

Example 6 is related to the lack of adequate purchasing data.

Failure to establish and maintain data that clearly describe or reference the specified requirement, including quality requirements, for purchased or otherwise received product and services, as required by 21 CFR 820.50(b).

Example 7 is related to the failure to establish and maintain adequate acceptance of incoming product. It's followed up with a response from the FDA stating that what the company provided was not adequate, nor did it confirm that prior material received followed proper receiving activities.

> Failure to establish and maintain adequate procedures for acceptance of incoming product, as required by 21 CFR 820.80(b).
>
> For example: According to Procedure 705, "Receiving," (b)(4) receiving acceptance activities are to be documented on a receiving log and approval documented on the packing slip. However, your firm has not developed or maintained a receiving log, and (b)(4) Packing Slips (b)(4) and (b)(4)) and (b)(4) Packing Lists (b)(4), and (b)(4) do not contain a signature and date for acceptance.
>
> We reviewed your firm's response and conclude that it is not adequate. Your firm promised to revise procedure 705 and develop a receiving log, but the response does not include that a new procedure, receiving log, or an evaluation of previously-received products to determine whether proper receiving acceptance activities were performed and that the received product was approved.

After Reviewing These Warning Letters . . .

Now that you've read these citings, the best advice is to review your internal systems to see if they are applicable. Walk through your processes and see if these citings apply to your current systems. Also, go over the GHTF flowchart in Figure 1.3 and see if your quality systems address these questions:

- Do gaps exist in my processes and/or procedures?
- Do my procedures follow a clear methodology regarding purchasing controls? Can I clearly explain the process to someone independent of my company?

Fill in Table 1.3 with your appropriate procedure number (or section within the document) and see how many areas need to be addressed.

Self-Assessment

Now that you've done this pass, try to go into more detail and answer the questions in "Self-Assessment Tool" provided on the CD accompanying this book.

Table 1.3 Self-assessment of your company's quality system to the GHTF elements.

Element	Your procedure number	Assessment
Planning		
Selection of potential supplier(s)		
Supplier evaluation and acceptance		
Finalization of controls		
Delivery, measurement, and monitoring		
Feedback and communication, including corrective action and preventive action process		

SUMMARY/TAKEAWAY

- Warning letters may and in fact do reflect purchasing control issues.
- Use the data to perform a gap assessment of your existing processes. The outcome can not only show areas that need to be addressed but provide a concise report outlining your process that can be shown to external parties.
- Purchasing controls is not "one size fits all"; it needs to be balanced based on the risk of your products and the controls you put in place based on the evaluation of your suppliers. Only you can determine that level.
- Don't create procedures that don't allow for various situations that you will encounter. However, there are some basic elements that have to be covered.

2
Planning: What Do We Need?

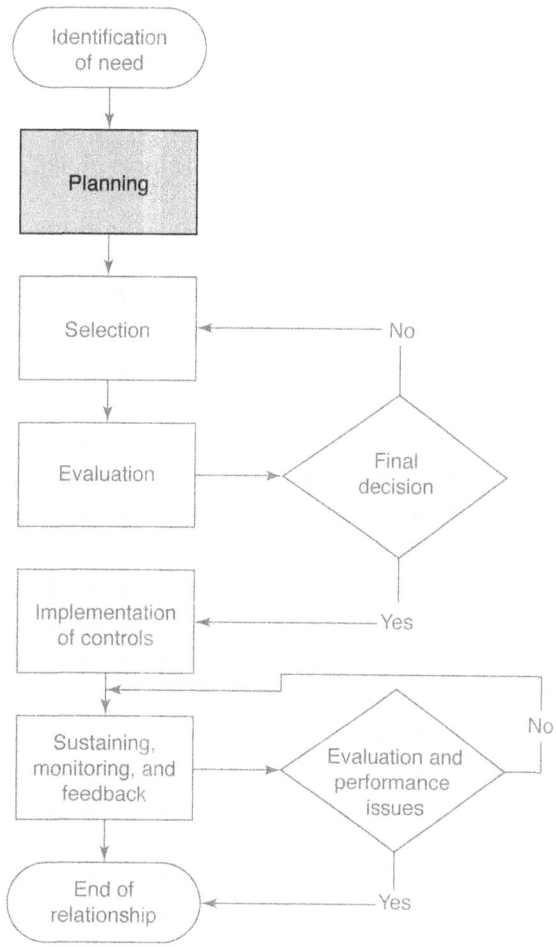

MAIN TOPICS COVERED IN THIS CHAPTER

1. How do you start the planning stage of supplier selection?
2. Who should be on the team and when?
3. How do you apply risk mitigation to supplier selection?

This chapter covers the following requirement from the FDA and ISO 13485:

> Sec. 820.50 Purchasing controls (a) Evaluation of suppliers, contractors, and consultants. Each manufacturer shall establish and maintain the requirements, including quality requirements, which must be met by suppliers, contractors, and consultants. Each manufacturer shall:
>
> (1) Evaluate and select potential suppliers, contractors, and consultants on the basis of their ability to meet specified requirements, including quality requirements. The evaluation shall be documented.

ISO 13485:2016 has very similar requirements with regard to evaluation of suppliers. The standard adds things like risk, reevaluation, and performance, whereas these can be found in the preamble to 820.

START WITH THE END IN MIND

When new models are presented, you expect to hear something like "That's great but it doesn't work at our company" or "We could never justify all those steps at our company." The intent of this book isn't to create a "one size fits all," but the framework or foundation to build upon that allows you to add what items you can implement and to develop the intensity that can be sustained. As quality professionals always say, "Incremental improvement is better than no improvement at all." Therefore, start with the basics and add what you can for your specific situation, product risk analysis, and your company.

BEFORE YOU GO TOO FAR . . .

What people sometimes forget is that the level of diligence that should be exercised should match the risk of the item being assessed. When assessing new sources, try to look at the commodity category, as shown in Table 2.1.

Your system should manage the amount of effort based on the higher-risk categories. For example, you may require very little for categories 3 and 4, as the impact of these suppliers is almost little to none.

Table 2.1 Example supplier category and risk rating.

Category	Risk level	Commodities
1	Critical or high	Contract manufacturers Outsourcing of software used in manufacturing
2	Medium	Precision components Printed circuit board assemblies
3	Low	Noncritical components Off-the-shelf items, noncritical
4	Negligible	Janitorial services Office supplies

START WITH YOUR ROAD MAP

A house must start with a strong foundation in order to support the structure and any future additions. As with any robust and repeatable process, structure and flexibility need to work together for a successful outcome. If the process is too rigid and can't handle exceptions, you will end up with an outcome that is not desirable. So, when starting a supplier selection process for new or existing suppliers, follow a road map to get to the best outcome.

This model takes the approach of "start with the end in mind" and builds on this premise and goal. The value this approach brings is the vision it will create to bring the team back in line when scope creep starts to show up. While it might be a good idea to add things to a project, the time line and scope of work can increase dramatically. Unless everyone agrees with this new direction, you could lose support and the team could lose its effectiveness. Figure 2.1 shows the next steps in the creation of this model.

FORM THE TEAM: WHO IS GOING TO PARTICIPATE?

Successful projects consist of properly sized project teams of the right subject matter experts along with the appropriate supply chain people. If you're going to find and select the right supplier, then you need people who have experience in that specific technical matter.

The size of the team may be determined by the size of your company. However, the recommendation is to limit it to no more than six people from, for example, engineering, purchasing, quality, or operations. The larger the group, the greater the tendency for it to turn into a committee that won't be able to make a decision—or worse, scope creep that doesn't allow the project to ever end.

You may bring in different people at different times based on the scope of the project and the expertise required for a specific task. For example, the financial analyst may only be needed in the project to review the supplier's financial stability. If certain members are not needed at a meeting, they will appreciate your letting them know that their presence is not required.

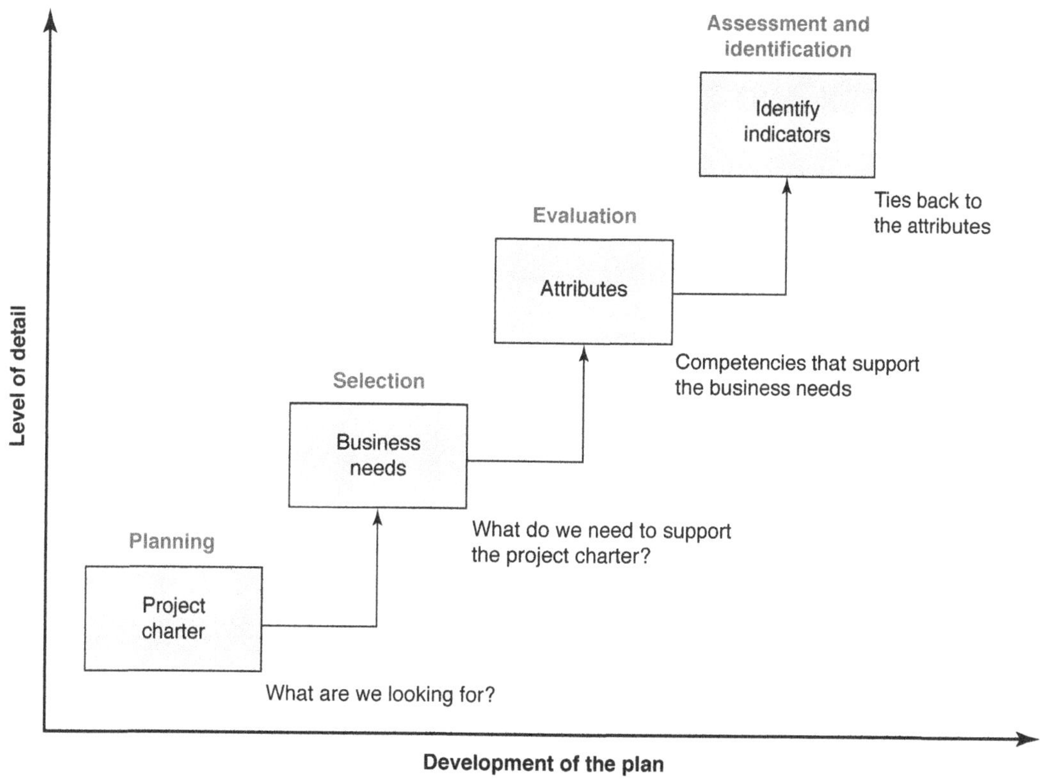

Figure 2.1 Example of supplier road map.

PLANNING—PROJECT CHARTER: WHAT ARE WE LOOKING FOR?

Once you have the right people, ask yourself what it is that you're trying to achieve. Without having a good focus, the project is in danger of having its scope changed or, worse, not getting done. Having a project charter will pay off later on when you see the team going off on a tangent or having issues with supplier selection. Consider the charter the GPS for the team. Just like a mission statement, the project charter states:

1. The specific outcome(s) you want to achieve
2. How success will be measured
3. The time line to complete the project

Here are some examples of a project charter (Table 2.2):

- "Contract Manufacturer (CM) that can partner with us in the development as well as the commercialization of a new, highly configurable catheter-based treatment device."
- "Metal and plastic machining supplier that can support our pilot product with quick turnaround requirements for the next six months as we build our new pressure controller."
- "Printed Circuit Board Assembly (PCBA) supplier that has the ability to reverse engineer our current design in order to document and assess the manufacturability. Once that is completed, the supplier needs to provide recommendations to upgrade from through-hole to surface-mount devices and meet the ROHS requirements."

The acronym SMART—specific, measurable, attainable, realistic, time bound—should be used to assess the charter. Spend the appropriate amount of time to make sure everyone on the team understands, agrees, and has buy-in to the charter.

Before going too much further, take a look at the team and make sure you've assembled the right individuals. If the technology or product scope has changed, you will need to make the necessary adjustments to the team.

SELECTION—BUSINESS NEEDS: WHAT DO WE NEED TO SUPPORT THE PROJECT CHARTER AND QUALITY REQUIREMENTS?

The business needs are derived from the project charter and provide the next level of detail of questions that need to be answered. What are the major elements or characteristics of a supplier that need to be in place in order to meet the charter and quality requirements?

For example, let's go back to the first charter in the list—"Contract Manufacturer (CM) that can partner with us in the development as well as the commercialization of a new, highly configurable catheter-based treatment device." Table 2.3 lists characteristics or traits that are needed by the supplier in order to meet the requirements of the charter for the contract manufacturer.

Table 2.2 Project charter and team.

Project Charter:
Contract manufacturer (CM) that can partner with us in the development as well as the commercialization of new highly configurable, catheter-based treatment device.
Project Team:
Project manager, supply chain, quality, R&D, catheter subject matter expert

Table 2.3 Business needs.

Business needs
Catheter development experience
Robust process development
Medium mix, high-volume manufacturing capacity
Regulatory experience
Medical device registered site
Robust quality system

The purpose of identifying these characteristics is not only to provide the next level of detail from the charter but to provide further guidelines. Furthermore, as you start reviewing suppliers you will have criteria to compare them.

This brainstorming session with the team is very important because it will help you further focus on the right suppliers as well as provide some alignment of the team. The activity allows others to hear what others on the team think is important. As you brainstorm, you may want to use sticky notes to capture all the ideas and then group them together (generally referred to as an affinity diagram). This will engage the team, and the project manager can see how everyone interacts with one another and in a group setting.

EVALUATION—ATTRIBUTES: WHAT ARE THE COMPETENCIES THAT SUPPORT THE BUSINESS NEEDS?

We create attributes that provide the specifics to further define the business needs. Each business need is reviewed, and this level of detail is an example of how the business need would

Table 2.4 Business needs and attributes.

Business need	Attributes
Catheter development experience	Past product development Appropriate equipment Expertise with process
Robust process development	Design for manufacturability Mistake proofing Simplified process steps
Medium mix, high-volume manufacturing capacity	Facility size Past experience with other products with multiple configurations Demand flow "pull" process
Regulatory experience	Personnel experienced with FDA product device submissions 510(k) submission experience
Medical device registered site	EN ISO certification Registered site with FDA
Robust quality system	Process controls (not inspection) Change management Electronic communications

be fulfilled. This structure allows suppliers to be compared and rated against each other (Table 2.4). Once the supplier assessment visits are performed, each person on the team can provide feedback and a rating on the same criteria (this will be further discussed in Chapter 3).

Caution about Rating Systems

Keep the values simple and on a small scale, like 1–3 (3 being excellent, 2 being acceptable, and 1 being not acceptable). Keeping the rating values small will allow you to keep the subjective evaluations from becoming distracting to the outcome. Once the team completes the assessment, collect the ratings on the attributes and look at the averages.

ASSESSMENT AND IDENTIFICATION—IDENTIFY INDICATORS: WHAT ATTRIBUTES ARE RELEVANT TO EACH BUSINESS NEED?

This level of detail is very similar to audit questions, which may or may not be required. The complexity of the supplier selection should dictate this level of questions. In most cases, these

Table 2.5 Business needs, attributes, and relevant indicators.

Business need	Attributes	Relevant indicators
Catheter development experience	Past product development Appropriate equipment Expertise with process	What products can you show us that demonstrate your ability to develop catheter-based products?
Robust process development	Design for manufacturability Mistake proofing Simplified process steps	Can you show us examples of the use of design for manufacturability? How do you assess products to this requirement?
Medium mix, high-volume manufacturing capacity	Facility size Past experience with other products with multiple configurations Demand flow "pull" process	Review of the site for these attributes
Regulatory experience	Personnel experienced with FDA product device submissions 510(k) submission experience	Who has been certified to the regulatory affairs certification per RAPS? What specific certification? What products are registered with the FDA and what is the product number?
Medical device registered site	EN ISO certification Registered site with FDA	Review site ISO certification Review http://www.accessdata.fda.gov/scripts/cdrh/cfdocs/cfRL/rl.cfm for supplier registration and any inspection reports if the supplier is required to be registered
Robust quality system FDA	Process controls (not inspection) Change management Electronic communications	What type of engineering change control process is used? How are changes communicated to the supplier, and are there certain types of changes that don't require customer approval?

questions are used as a guideline or to prompt the assessment team for questions that should be asked to assess the supplier against the attributes (Table 2.5).

FDA Change control and quality agreements are critical to supplier management. (Refer to FDA 21 CFR 820.50(b) and 801.150(e)(1), which explain the details of the regulations. Chapter 5 provides more details regarding change management.)

OBJECTIVE EVIDENCE

Table 2.6 is an example of the form that can be used to document the planning phase of the supplier selection process. The form is also provided on the CD accompanying this book.

THE FINISHED PRODUCT

Table 2.7 shows the completed road map for this project.

SUMMARY/TAKEAWAY

- Start the planning stage of supplier selection with a project charter that includes quality requirements. This is the "GPS" of the project and will help you navigate the process and identify changes to the scope.
- Bring individuals on the team as you need them, and ask them to attend meetings as needed. Be cognizant of their time.
- Use the commodity type to determine what controls are needed based on risk mitigation. The same intensity of evaluation should not be applied to a contract manufacturer of a complex system as that applied to the supplier of a manufacturing aid.
- Apply supplier controls appropriately based on the outcome of the supplier evaluation and the risk profile.

Table 2.6 Supplier selection road map.

Project charter:			
Team members:			
#	**Business need**	**Attributes**	**Relevant indicators**

Table 2.7 Completed supplier selection road map.

Project charter: Contract manufacturer (CM) that can partner with us in the development as well as the commercialization of new highly configurable catheter-based treatment device.

Team members: Supply chain, quality assurance, development engineer, manufacturing engineer

#	Business need	Attributes	Relevant indicators
1	Catheter development experience	Past product development Appropriate equipment Expertise with process	What products can you show us that demonstrate your ability to develop catheter-based products?
2	Robust process development	Design for manufacturability Mistake proofing Simplified process steps	Can you show us examples of the use of design for manufacturability? How do you assess products to this requirement?
3	Medium mix, high-volume manufacturing capacity	Facility size Past experience with other products with multiple configurations Demand flow "pull" process	Review of the site for these attributes
4	Regulatory experience	Personnel experienced with FDA product device submissions 510(k) submission experience	Who has been certified to the Regulatory Affairs Certification per RAPS? What specific certification? What products are registered with the FDA and what is the product number?
5	Medical device registered site	EN ISO certification Registered site with FDA	Review site ISO certification Review http://www.accessdata.fda.gov/scripts/cdrh/cfdocs/cfRL/rl.cfm for supplier registration and any inspection reports if the supplier is required to be registered
6	Robust quality system	Process controls (not inspection) Change management Electronic communications	What type of engineering change control process is used? How are changes communicated to the supplier, and are there certain types of changes that don't require customer approval?

3

Selection of Suppliers: Which Ones Do We Need?

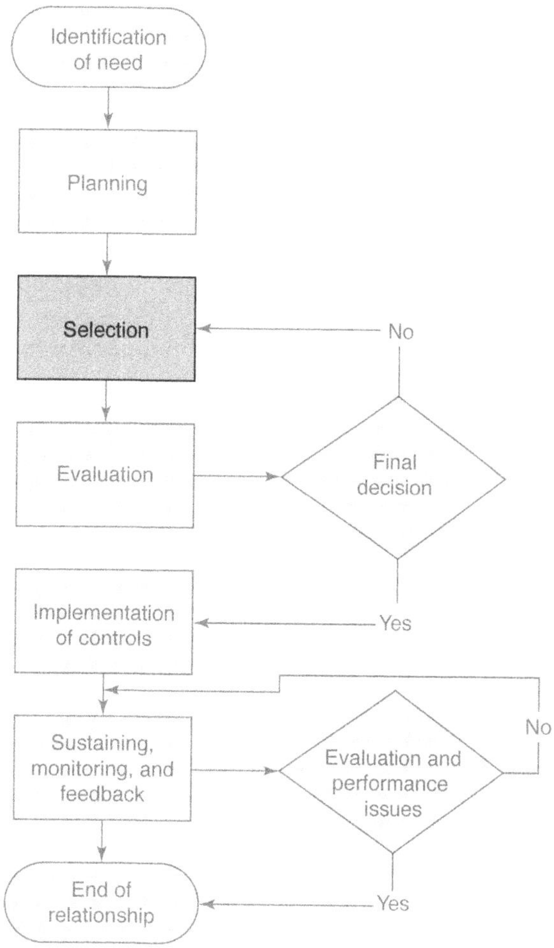

Once the need has been identified to outsource a product based on your planning stage, as discussed in the previous chapter, the next part of the process is to conduct supplier selection and eventually an evaluation of the supplier(s) you wish to engage with further.

MAIN TAKEAWAYS FROM THIS CHAPTER

- The time spent planning the selection of a supplier will be time well spent. The work done in the previous chapter provides the foundation for this part of the process.
- You will learn how to use the Total Risk Factor (TRF) to compare suppliers based on risk factors.
- The flexibility of the system is critical in order to be an effective process and one everyone can follow. Identify elements that you can use in your company effectively and consistently. Keeping it simple and sustainable is key!
- This is the step within the process where you should have an onboarding process for suppliers.
- Control plans should be drafted as well at this point.

This chapter covers the following requirement from the FDA and ISO 13485:

> Sec. 820.50 Purchasing controls. Each manufacturer shall establish and maintain procedures to ensure that all purchased or otherwise received product and services conform to specified requirements.
>
> (a) *Evaluation of suppliers, contractors, and consultants.* Each manufacturer shall establish and maintain the requirements, including quality requirements that must be met by suppliers, contractors, and consultants. Each manufacturer shall:
>
> (1) Evaluate and select potential suppliers, contractors, and consultants on the basis of their ability to meet specified requirements, including quality requirements. The evaluation shall be documented.

As stated in Chapter 1, since the ISO standard is protected under copyright laws, we have paraphrased the requirements in ISO 13485:2016. Similar to the FDA's requirements for purchasing controls, the ISO states you shall evaluate and select suppliers based on:

- Requirements meeting your needs
- The supplier's performance
- How the quality of the purchased product may affect the finished device
- Risk commensurate with the product or service

It should be noted that not all suppliers you consider in your initial assessment will advance to a more thorough evaluation, but all these records should be maintained for future reference in the event that suppliers not meeting your criteria are considered for future opportunities. It never fails that someone will recommend a supplier that you've already excluded for good reasons but which were not written down. The outcome is that you'll waste time repeating this evaluation.

TYPE OF PRODUCT OR SERVICE OBTAINED: USING RISK IN SELECTION OF SUPPLIERS

What people sometimes forget is that the level of diligence that should be exercised should match the risk of the item being assessed. When assessing new sources, try to look at the commodity category, as shown in Table 3.1.

Your system should manage the amount of effort based on the higher-risk categories. If you are able to implement these commodity categories, it will greatly help you justify the intensity and effort put toward the category 1 and 2 suppliers.

Table 3.1 Example supplier category and risk rating.

Category	Risk level	Commodities
1	Critical or high	Contract manufacturers Outsourcing of software used in manufacturing
2	Medium	Precision components Printed circuit board assemblies
3	Low	Noncritical components Off-the-shelf items, noncritical
4	Negligible	Janitorial services Office supplies

Whether to identify category 4 suppliers in the quality management system is something you have to decide. We recommend identifying the "noncritical suppliers" for the following reasons:

- In the true sense that they are in fact suppliers but are not identified as noncritical, the company could easily end up with an audit finding or 483 observation.
- These suppliers can be easily tagged in the database with this category, which allows them to be filtered out from the approved supplier list.

Within your internal procedures, we recommend stating that "Category 4 suppliers do not impact the quality management system and are not maintained on the approved supplier list."

What Table 3.2 will allow the team to do is to agree on what level of intensity needs to be applied during this assessment. Based on the risk assigned to the product commodity, the level of controls can be defined as shown in Table 3.2.

Table 3.2 Example of ongoing supplier monitoring.

Category	Risk level	Commodities	Controls
1	Critical or high	Finished medical devices Contract manufacturers Outsourcing of software used in manufacturing	Quarterly/annual assessments Dun & Bradstreet reporting Process control plans Incoming inspection plans
2	Medium	Precision components Printed circuit board assemblies	Annual assessments Dun & Bradstreet reporting Process control plans Incoming inspection plans
3	Low	Noncritical components Off-the-shelf items, noncritical	On-site assessments every two to three years (if necessary) Incoming inspection plans Supplier survey provided by the supplier
4	Negligible	Janitorial services for nonmanufacturing areas Office supplies	Paper survey provided by the supplier Monitoring based on areas that are serviced

If you take this approach, make sure you document that for certain categories no activities are required other than getting the basic approval of the purchasing manager. If other activities are required to update the approved supplier list (ASL) or some other list, make sure to include them as well. These little details usually end up in an audit finding or 483 observation if not documented, which then leads to more detailed questions. We'll discuss ASLs and controls in more detail in later chapters.

SUPPLIER SELECTION ACTIVITIES

Whether the supplier is a current or a new supplier, multiple suppliers should be considered in the initial assessment based on the required criteria developed in the planning phase. The process can start with an internet search, trade shows, trade magazines, phone calls to potential suppliers, or recommendations from a reliable source.

From a "total cost of ownership," current suppliers should be considered before adding additional suppliers. If your process requires annual audits, a new supplier will increase your annual cost for travel and resources. However, business and performance considerations should be reviewed before making that decision.

There are a multitude of attributes a company should consider when selecting suppliers to evaluate, and they should reflect the risk associated with the service to be provided. Having this list of attributes prior to selecting and evaluating suppliers will allow you to compare multiple suppliers in the form of a scorecard. Again, the FDA doesn't tell you how to select suppliers; it's expected that your company will create the process and demonstrate the effectiveness. Each product and service should be evaluated on a case-by-case basis and not a "one size fits all" for a given supplier supplying multiple products or services.

This point is further supported by Kim Trautman (2012, p. 6), former associate director for international affairs, Office of the Center Director, and FDA's Medical Device International Quality Systems Expert.

> Same supplied product or service may have different risks based on use.
>
> Same supplier may have different risks for different supplied product or service.
>
> - Quality Management System Maturity
>   - Age of QMS
>   - Sr. Management tenure with company
> - Supplier Culture
>   - People happy about going to work
>   - Do they have a revolving door
> - Selection Criteria
>   - Operational capability
>   - Business capability
> - Risk (recall from planning)
>   - Product risk (severity, effect on end user)
>   - Business risk (not the primary factor, but something to consider for long term relationships)
> - Supplier's Presence
>   - Local
>   - Global

- Supplier's Quality System Detection
- Financial Stress Factor (viability)
- Order Capacity (% of your business)
- Lead-time
- Regulatory Compliance Profile

If the company is registered with the FDA, the company's regulatory compliance status as well as other information can be reviewed by conducting a search on the FDA's website (http://www.accessdata.fda.gov/scripts/cdrh/cfdocs/cfRL/rl.cfm).

Whatever method you use, the more formal assessment (also known as the "deep dive") should be conducted with what was obtained during your initial assessment. One way to get more information is to provide the supplier with a list of questions and have them return it with the appropriate information. In addition to the questions you identified during your supplier selection road map from the previous chapter, here are some additional areas to consider:

- Logistics
- Quality
- Manufacturing
- Training
- Distribution—geared toward off-the-shelf parts

The supplier survey appears on the CD accompanying this book. Make sure to modify it so it can be used consistently at your company, rather than using some other company's procedure that can't be followed or does not fit the requirements needed for your product or business needs.

Once this initial information about each supplier is gathered, the suppliers can then be compared against one another and the suppliers that have an overall low risk could be evaluated further. The following exercise illustrates use of the TRF initial assessment.

Before you start asking for information from suppliers, make sure the team agrees with the indicators that identify the best supplier. Sometimes emotions and egos get in the way of making the best selection because of an earlier underlying conflict between a supplier and someone on the team.

USING RISK THE RIGHT WAY: TRF

Over the years we have seen various supplier rating forms that have ranged from very complex systems to very simple systems. We believe that keeping it simple will prevent diluting the end result and allow you to apply the appropriate rating for your supplier. This will also allow you to define the type and extent of controls needed based on the evaluation.

The following is a method of how to use both product risk and business risk to conduct an initial assessment of multiple suppliers. In this example, the following criteria will be used for an initial assessment of three individual suppliers, and the supplier with the overall lowest TRF will be evaluated further with the intent to engage the supplier or suppliers for future business.

Factors that can be used to determine the lowest TRF are as follows:

- Severity of the product/service being provided
- Supplier's quality system detection

- Financial stress factor (viability)
- Order capacity (percentage of your business)
- Lead time
- Indicators identified in the previous chapter

WAIT, I THOUGHT RISK MANAGEMENT WAS USED ONLY IN DESIGN AND PROCESS FMEAS?

One of the best and most common tools used for determining the risk associated with a component or finished medical device in the medical device industry is a design failure mode and effects analysis (design FMEA). So why can't we apply this to supplier selection?

Industry feedback in the preamble to 21 CFR 820, comment #115, points out that "the need for specifications should be based on the criticality of and risk associated with the use of the specific manufacturing material." The FDA furthers this comment by stating, "The extent of the specification detail necessary to ensure that the product or service purchased meets requirements will be related to the nature of the product or service purchased, taking into account the effect the product or service may have on the safety or effectiveness of the finished device."

FACTOR: PRODUCT SEVERITY

Table 3.3 is an example of ranking the severity of a product. The scale has been reduced to include only 2, 4, 6, 8, and 10 to help reduce some of the potential conflicts that occur from, for example, selecting either 3 or 4. If you have a severity ranking from your risk management plan that is different from what is listed here, pick the higher value for the evaluation. The severity for each supplier will be the same during your initial assessment, as it's related to the product being purchased or otherwise received.

The example in Table 3.4 walks you through initially assessing multiple suppliers in order to select the best suppliers based on the criteria selected; the severity of the component will be given an 8.

Table 3.3 Design FMEA severity table.

Effect	Criteria: Severity of effect	Ranking
Hazardous	Very high severity ranking when a potential failure mode affects safe product operation. Noncompliance with government regulations. Patient death.	10
High	Product inoperable, with loss of primary function. Customer very dissatisfied.	8
Moderate	Product operable, but nonessential system inoperable. Customer experiences discomfort or dissatisfaction.	6
Low	Fit and finish does not conform. Defect noticed by most customers.	4
Minor to none	Fit and finish does not conform. Defect noticed by discriminating (<25%) customers, or no effect	2

Table 3.4 Example TRF assessment criteria form with severity populated.

Supplier	Severity (dFMEA)	Supplier QS detection	Financial strength	Lead time	Order capacity	TRF
Supplier A	8					
Supplier B	8					
Supplier C	8					

FACTOR: SUPPLIER'S QUALITY SYSTEM DETECTION

Using a format much like an FMEA table, you can rank the supplier's quality detection based on the type of process it has in place. Over the 20+ years of auditing suppliers, it's been our observation that most suppliers fall into the ranking of 4 or 6, with a bell-shaped distribution curve that skews slightly toward doing more in process controls. Today it is rare that a supplier has no quality system at all or does 100% inspection all the time.

Unless you plan on doing 100% incoming inspection, you will have a high reliance on the supplier's quality system detection process. It's very critical that you understand the type of detection your supplier is capable of achieving. This can range from no inspection at some level of controls to a 100% validated automated in-line inspection system that rejects nonconforming product on the spot. This is where the process will begin to vary based on the supplier's maturity level. Use Table 3.5 as a guide when selecting the supplier's quality system detection.

At the time you start the supplier selection, you may not have a ranking of the supplier's quality detection system. We recommend you start with making it equal across the board using a ranking of 4, and then update it after you complete either your desktop or your on-site assessment.

For the example in Table 3.6, we are considering three existing suppliers already on our ASL and have conducted on-site assessments.

Table 3.5 Example of supplier quality system detection.

Detection	Criteria	Suggested range of detection method	Ranking
Almost impossible	Quality system (QS) will not and/or cannot detect a potential cause/mechanism and subsequent failure mode.	None; no QS in place.	10
Low	QS has a poor chance of detecting a potential cause/mechanism and subsequent failure mode.	Indirect/infrequent checks only.	8
Moderate	QS may detect a potential cause/mechanism and subsequent failure mode.	Visual checks and measurements/gauging components. Periodic charting and tracking.	6
High	QS has a good chance to detect potential cause/mechanism and subsequent failure mode.	Measurements/gauging or testing/sampling of components during production to prevent potential failures. Continuous charting and tracking.	4
Almost certain	QS almost certain to detect potential cause/mechanism and subsequent failure mode.	Continuous monitoring predicts potential failures prior to occurrence.	2

Table 3.6 Example TRF assessment form with supplier QS detection populated.

Supplier	Severity (dFMEA)	Supplier QS detection	Financial strength	Lead time	Order capacity	TRF
Supplier A	8	6				
Supplier B	8	2				
Supplier C	8	4				

FACTOR: SUPPLIER'S FINANCIAL STRENGTH

You might ask why it's important to understand the financial aspect of the company, as this has no bearing on product quality. However, the financial strength has a great influence on the quality management of the supplier. If the supplier has cash flow issues and is on credit hold with its suppliers, items such as calibration services could be impacted (pushed out or not done at all). This is purely a business risk that should be evaluated, especially if the company is fairly new and a new supplier to your company. You want to gain some level of assurance that the company you plan to do business with will be around for at least the life of the product being built. This plays a big role in the regulatory submission and approval of your product and the impact of having to change a supplier.

Table 3.7 is an example of a financial stress factor taken from Dun & Bradstreet. The financial strength (or financial stress score, as referred to by Dun & Bradstreet) predicts the likelihood of business failure over the next 12 months. If there is no rating on Dun & Bradstreet for the supplier, use your best judgment as a means of a rating if you plan to use the financial stress factor as part of your business risk. If your company uses a different means to assess the supplier's financial viability, you will need to modify your tool based on that rating. One word of caution about using Dun & Bradstreet ratings is that information is provided by the company to Dun & Bradstreet.

Continuing with our example of the initial assessment of the three suppliers, the finance department was able to find the following information on these selected suppliers:

Supplier A financial strength factor = 2

Supplier B financial strength factor = 3

Supplier C financial strength factor = 5

Table 3.7 Example of financial stress factor.

Financial stress risk class	Financial stress score
1	1316–1875
2	1288–1315
3	1255–1287
4	1216–1254
5	1001–1215

Source: Modified from Dun & Bradstreet, "Distribution of Financial Stress Class," https://na3.dnbi.com/help/sas_help/glossary.html#f.

Table 3.8 Example TRF assessment form with financial strength populated.

Supplier	Severity (dFMEA)	Supplier QS detection	Financial strength	Lead time	Order capacity	TRF
Supplier A	8	6	2			
Supplier B	8	2	3			
Supplier C	8	4	5			

This is one of the reasons you need finance as part of your cross-functional team supporting supplier selection. We've always found it's best to rely on this department's expertise to review financial data and to provide the financial strength factor. See Table 3.8 for the financial stress factor added to the TRF.

FACTOR: LEAD TIME

Lead time and the ability to respond to increases (and decreases) in business needs is a critical quality factor to consider in supplier selection. To reduce lead time, most suppliers have adopted lean manufacturing principles and have implemented some form of kanban or finished product inventory to make sure the shipment dates are made. These methods are important for understanding how much inventory the supplier has in the facility at any time. In the case of a quality issue, there may be issues with screening and sorting large amounts of inventory, which might impact the current scheduled deliveries.

In Table 3.9 the days are used only as an example and should be modified for each situation. In our example, the three suppliers are existing suppliers; their delivery performance has been tracked for several years, and the values are just for demonstration purposes. If you don't have any past history, we suggest you use the highest lead time factor of the other supplier being compared and document your rationale in the notes. If someone asks you why you selected this value, you can offer an explanation from your notes. Table 3.10 shows the TRF populated with the lead time.

Table 3.9 Example of lead time.

Risk factor	Lead-time criteria
1	≤3 days
2	4–6 days
3	7 or 8 days
4	9 or 10 days
5	>10 days

Table 3.10 Example TRF assessment form with supplier lead time populated.

Supplier	Severity (dFMEA)	Supplier QS detection	Financial strength	Lead time	Order capacity	TRF
Supplier A	8	6	2	**4**		
Supplier B	8	2	3	**2**		
Supplier C	8	4	5	**3**		

FACTOR: ORDER CAPACITY

The final criterion that was chosen for this example was order capacity, as displayed in Table 3.11. Order capacity as used in this example is how much of the supplier's business your company will have in annual revenue. For this example the supplier was penalized for too much reliance on the company for business. However, this can be flipped if your company desires to have more focus from your suppliers, particularly for critical components or a finished medical device being outsourced to a contract manufacturer.

The rule of thumb that you never want to be more than 20% of anyone's business should be considered but may not always apply. If you have a sole source supplier, you may not be able to change that situation. However, this exercise should highlight the risk. Make sure you have the necessary mitigation strategy in place.

The form is filled in based on the current suppliers and the knowledge you have from your current business relationship. If you don't have this information at the time you are starting the evaluation, we recommend using the default value of 3 and modifying it after you finish the evaluation. See Table 3.12, which shows the order capacity being added.

INITIAL TRF: BASIC APPROACH

Now that you've filled in the form, all you need to do is add the values across to identify the TRF for each supplier, as displayed in Table 3.13.

This basic approach will help you see the bigger picture with the minimal effort to reach it. It's obvious that supplier B is the best choice when using the TRF value.

Table 3.11 Example of order capacity.

Risk factor	Order capacity
1	<15%
3	15%–25%
5	>25%

Table 3.12 Example TRF assessment form with order capacity populated.

Supplier	Severity (dFMEA)	Supplier QS detection	Financial strength	Lead time	Order capacity	TRF
Supplier A	8	6	2	4	1	
Supplier B	8	2	3	2	1	
Supplier C	8	4	5	3	1	

Table 3.13 Example TRF assessment form populated.

Supplier	Severity (dFMEA)	Supplier QS detection	Financial strength	Lead time	Order capacity	TRF
Supplier A	8	6	2	4	1	21
Supplier B	8	2	3	2	1	16
Supplier C	8	4	5	3	1	21

The results are very interesting, as you can see that one supplier shows the lowest value, while two suppliers have the same value. Supplier B seems to be the clear winner regarding the lowest TRF, but this is based on the premise that everything is equally important. This is one of the weaknesses of systems that are one-dimensional.

INITIAL TRF: WEIGHTED APPROACH

If the basic approach gets you to where you need to be, then you don't need to take it any further. However, for a small investment of time you can get better information to make a better decision. The weighted approach uses the premise that not everything is as important as everything else. Jim's great mentor and friend Steve Perez would often say the old adage "If everything is a priority, then nothing is a priority." The advantage of the weighted approach is that the value can be changed to fit your needs, so it provides not only structure but also flexibility.

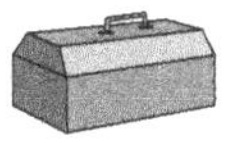

Table 3.14 can be created in Microsoft Excel based on the example we have provided. We have also included the tool as part of the CD material if you wish to make modifications to fit your particular situation.

We recommend that you weight the individual criteria, giving preference to product risks having higher weighting values than those of the business risks. Again, this is modified based on your company's acceptance of risk and commensurate with the risk of the product. In this example the following weights were applied to each of the criteria:

- Severity = 1.5
- Supplier quality system (QS) detection = 0.75
- Financial strength factor = 1
- Lead time = 0.5
- Order capacity = 0.25

To calculate the TRF for each criterion, first multiply the severity value and weight value and then sum all the values. For example, in Table 3.15 the product was given a severity

Table 3.14 TRF assessment criteria form, weighted approach.

	Severity (dFMEA)			Supplier QS detection			Financial strength			Lead time			Order capacity			
Supplier	S	Weight value	Risk	D	Weight value	Risk	F	Weight value	Risk	LT	Weight value	Risk	OC	Weight value	Risk	TRF
A	8			6			2			4			1			
B	8			2			3			2			1			
C	8			4			5			3			1			

Table 3.15 Combined initial supplier assessment rating.

	Severity (dFMEA)			Supplier QS detection			Financial strength			Lead time			Order capacity			
Supplier	S	Weight value	Risk	D	Weight value	Risk	F	Weight value	Risk	LT	Weight value	Risk	OC	Weight value	Risk	TRF
A	8	1.5	12	6	0.75	4.5	2	1	2	4	0.5	2.0	1	0.25	0.25	**20.75**
B	8	1.5	12	2	0.75	1.5	3	1	3	2	0.5	1.0	1	0.25	0.25	**17.75**
C	8	1.5	12	4	0.75	3	5	1	5	3	0.5	1.5	1	0.25	0.25	**21.75**

value of 8 and a weight value of 1.5, for a total risk of 12 for our criterion of severity. The process repeats itself until all individual risks are calculated and the sum of the individual risks equals the TRF. So for supplier A, the sum of 12, 4.5, 2, 2, and 0.25 equals 20.75.

INITIAL TRF (WEIGHTED APPROACH): ANALYSIS

When we first looked at these suppliers using the basic method, supplier B clearly had the lowest TRF rating and supplier A and supplier C were tied. Now when you look at the TRF rating, supplier B is still the lowest risk, but supplier A is different from supplier C. The additional information should help you determine that if you only wanted to look at one supplier but have a backup, then supplier B would be the primary and supplier A would be the backup.

From the example illustrated, supplier B has the lowest overall risk and is the one that you would want to conduct further evaluation with first. This could be followed up with supplier A, or both could be done at the same time if there's a possibility you would like to have one as a backup supplier.

One thing to remember is to review why there is a difference and to check your assumptions. In this case, the big difference was the financial strength factor. Though supplier A's QS detection was not as good as supplier C's, the financial factor was the three-point difference. Now is a good time to go back and verify that the information regarding the supplier's financial situation is correct; if you are currently doing business with the supplier, you should take a look at the risk that exists right now. Is it having cash flow problems? Did it lose other business that is affecting its financial analysis? Is it in the middle of expanding its facility?

Please note that the process of how to determine which suppliers are to be formally evaluated is not a requirement of the QSReg; anything you document as part of your process becomes a process that can be subject to investigation by the agency.

INITIAL TRF: RECOMMENDED ACTIONS

After calculating the TRF, you should have recommended actions to take based on the TRF score. The TRF score will change based on the number of criteria you've selected and on the weighted value you've applied to each criterion. Again, this process is to help you eliminate unacceptable suppliers in your initial supplier assessment in order to focus on the vitally few suppliers you wish to evaluate further. We recommend that you save your initial assessment of all suppliers, even the unacceptable suppliers, in the event you wish to reconsider the supplier after it has implemented changes to improve its quality system.

Table 3.16 lists examples of recommended actions based on each supplier's TRF. The TRFs illustrated in this example are based on the five criteria initially selected. If more or less

Table 3.16 TRF recommended action.

Total risk factor	Recommended action
TRF ≥ 25	Either avoid supplier or use the most extreme level of control. Examples: Person in the plant monitoring day-to-day activities or releasing product, 100% receiving inspection (RI), 100% inline inspection/testing during your assembly, continuous supplier monitoring, excessive inventory buffer, backup supplier, probation period, continuous monitoring of supplier's financial status.
20 ≤TRF> 25	High to moderate risk for selection/level of control associated with supplier. Examples: Use of tightened to normal RI, ongoing supplier monitoring, moderate inventory buffer; could consider single source supplier, frequent monitoring of supplier's financial status.
TRF < 20	Moderate to low risk for selection/control of supplier. Examples: Use of normal to reduced RI, periodic supplier monitoring, use as single source supplier, light to no inventory buffer.

criteria are selected, your threshold for each recommendation will need to change based on your selection criteria. As previously stated, this is one method of eliminating unacceptable suppliers in your initial assessment so you can focus on acceptable suppliers to further evaluate. With the limited number of resources that we have available today, it is highly recommended that you develop some form of initial screening when you have multiple suppliers that could potentially provide product. If your company already has a method to initially screen multiple suppliers, consider doing an assessment of your process to see if it's adequate and is being used and not bypassed.

As stated previously, supplier B would get evaluated further, while supplier A would be placed in a holding pattern if for some reason supplier B did not work out. Supplier C should be avoided unless you use the most extreme controls over the supplier.

ONBOARDING YOUR POTENTIAL SUPPLIERS

What internal processes need to be addressed in order to do business with your new suppliers? Now is the time to start thinking about these items and use a checklist to make sure they get accomplished. For example, here's a list of items you should consider:

- Nondisclosure agreement
- Supplier information required for your order entry system (material requirements planning)
- Supplier is set up in the financial accounts payable system

PROCESS CONTROL AND QUALITY CONTROL PLANS

By this time, quality and engineering should have created the preliminary process control plan and quality control plan. Both tools accomplish the mission, but for consistency purposes within the book, we will refer to process control plans (PCPs). If this is an existing item, the plan should be reviewed to make sure it's current and has addressed all of the current performance issues.

PCPs are most effective when the requirements are based on the risk management process, which specifically would be either the design FMEA or other hazard analysis tools. The priority of the highest risk (severity and occurrence) should be identified on the plan and the proposed controls should be identified.

This should be shared with the supplier along with an explanation of where the priorities come from so the supplier can understand and implement the correct controls. There are too many times that the drawing or specification is given to the supplier without any explanation regarding the failure modes and severity. Without knowing the importance, and having only half the information, how can the supplier be successful?

Chapter 5 provides more details on process control plans.

SUMMARY/TAKEAWAY

- The work conducted during planning and selection can be a feeder into the TRF assessment. These activities are building blocks to the next process step, which should not be skipped.
- Remember, "plagiarism is the best form of flattery, but poor implementation of a good idea is just plain bad." So, before you make these steps mandatory within your quality system, perform a pilot test to work out the bugs.

- Onboarding suppliers is just like bringing new employees into the company. Make sure you are ready to spend the appropriate amount of time to help them be successful right from the beginning.
- Have your PCP ready and explain the "mission critical" items.

WHAT'S NEXT?

- At this point you may have identified suppliers you want to evaluate further as well as suppliers you are not going to consider at this time.
- You have assigned a weighted risk factor to create a risk profile for each supplier.
- You may need to get more information to make a better decision.

4

Evaluation: Do They Meet Our Needs?

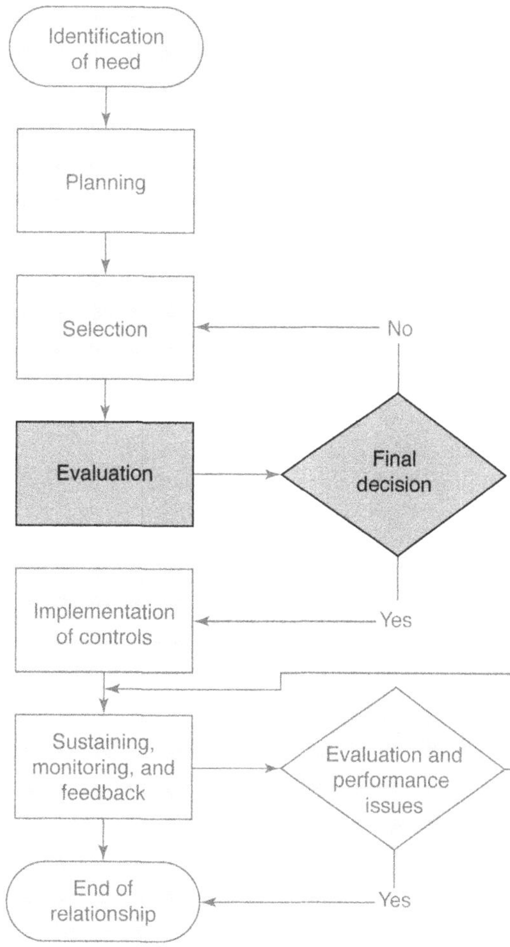

Now we come to the fun part—going to meet the supplier and conduct the on-site evaluation. The work you did in the previous chapter scoped out the initial assessment of suppliers you want to engage with further. Your initial assessment has eliminated potential suppliers not meeting your initial assessment criteria; a more thorough supplier evaluation needs to be conducted with the remaining supplier(s)—aka "the deep dive."

MAIN TAKEAWAYS FROM THIS CHAPTER

- The work done in previous chapters will allow this evaluation to be done with better outcomes
- The evaluations will not only allow you to compare each supplier against the requirements but compare them with with one another.
- The outcome can be documented and is easily defendable in front of any external agency or customer.

WHAT WILL NOT BE PART OF THIS CHAPTER?

The actual audit techniques will not be part of this book, as there are too many resources and techniques to combine into this one chapter. We feel our competency is helping you put together the supplier quality management system, and we would only be rehashing items you already know how to do.

An audit checklist that can be modified to your needs is included on the CD accompanying this book. However, the work done during the prior process steps should be prioritized to make sure "relevant indicators" is answered.

FDA

Within 21 CFR 820.50

Each manufacturer shall establish and maintain procedures to ensure that all purchased or otherwise received product and services conform to specified requirements.

(a) Evaluation of suppliers, contractors, and consultants. Each manufacturer shall establish and maintain the requirements, including quality requirements, that must be met by suppliers, contractors, and consultants. Each manufacturer shall:

(1) Evaluate and select potential suppliers, contractors, and consultants on the basis of their ability to meet specified requirements, including quality requirements. The evaluation shall be documented.

Preamble to the 1996 QS Regulation, Comment #99

Where audits are not practical, this may be done through, among other means, reviewing historical data, monitoring and trending, and inspection and testing.

PROCESS STEPS

As engineers we view most things by starting with a process flowchart. Figure 4.1 shows the steps you should consider for conducting your evaluation. The approach is flexible, so you may use it to make sure you cover each item, similar to a checklist.

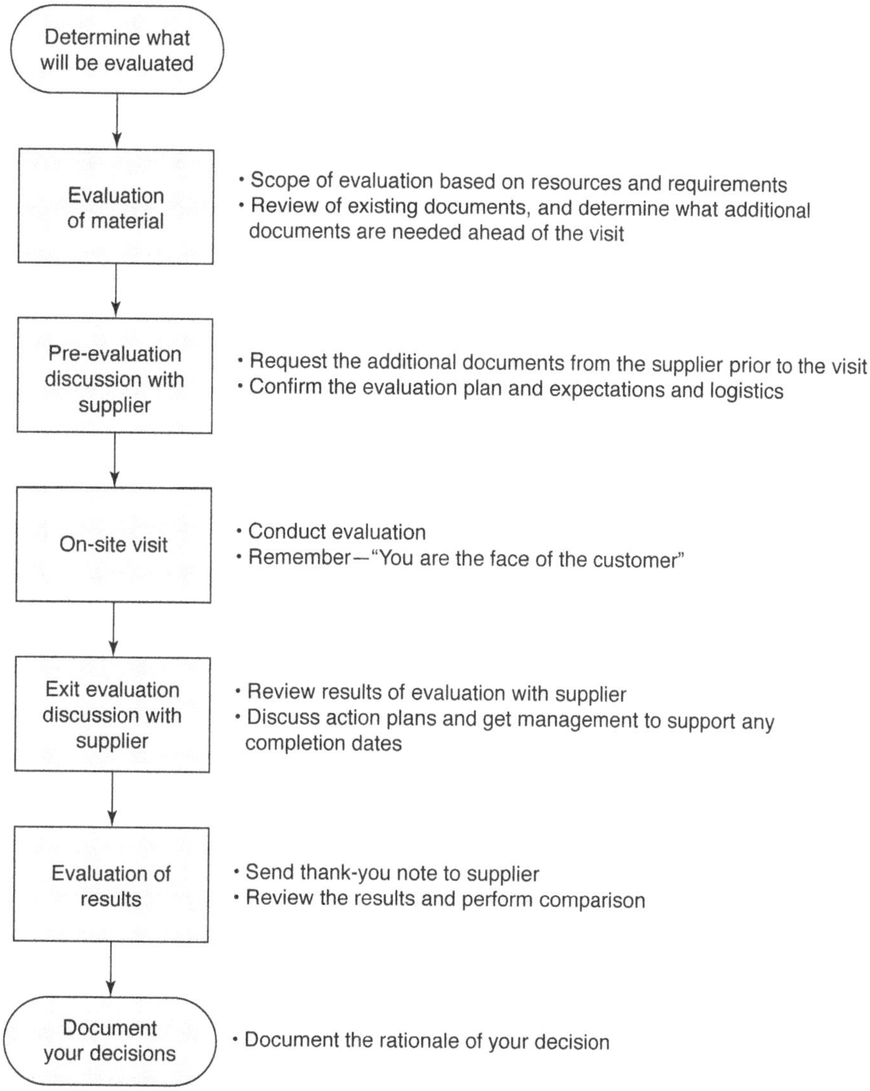

Figure 4.1 Process flow for performing an evaluation at a supplier.

DETERMINE WHAT WILL BE EVALUATED

At this point, you have identified the supplier(s) that you will further evaluate either on-site or through a desktop assessment. All of the information that you've collected in the previous process steps should be used to determine your evaluation. Before going further, ask the potential supplier to fill out a brief survey to get more details. We have provided a sample supplier survey form on the CD accompanying this book to help you create your own form or to verify that your existing one has the appropriate elements. Please note that a consultant survey should be different from the supplier survey and may be better as a separate document since you will be looking more at the credentials of the individual consultant as opposed to the processes of the manufacturer.

Some of the key elements that should be part of the supplier survey are as follows:

- Key people within the organization—general manager; individuals who work in quality, manufacturing, or customer service
- Minority/veteran status

- Private versus public owned
- Union workforce
- Percentage of business that is focused on the medical device industry
- Total number of employees broken out by function
- Basic quality, logistics, manufacturing, and operations questions (see survey on the CD accompanying this book)

This survey should not be difficult or time-consuming to complete. "Smart forms," online forms, or simple checkboxes should be used to help make this easy for the supplier. A general rule of thumb is to do the work and then verify. Fill in the checklist and then ask yourself, was that difficult or did it take long to do? If the answer is yes, then simplify it.

EVALUATION OF MATERIAL

After receiving the completed survey and deciding to move forward with this supplier, you may want to ask the supplier for a list of documents prior to the visit so you can be better prepared:

- Quality manual and any applicable certifications (ISO, CE, UL)
- List of procedures and work instructions
- A specific work instruction you want to read in more detail
- A copy of the process control plan templates that are currently used in the facility

In Chapter 2 we created a planning document for supplier selection. If those steps were followed we would recommend outlining those attributes and relevant indicators as part of your evaluation. One item that we would recommend at this time is to create a scale that provides a standard method to compare suppliers with suppliers. The criteria can be a simple checklist of items or a scale of 1–3:

1 = benchmarking processes

2 = compliant systems

3 = concerns of effectiveness

No matter the metric, it's important that it's established with the other functional groups involved in your company prior to the visit. The reasoning is that it will remove any subjectivity from the outcome, especially when other people are involved. This is very common since we may view the situation differently based on our experience and expertise.

Again, the TRF model shown in Table 4.1 is one way to utilize the ranking as well as the weighted values that were discussed in the prior chapter. This may help with taking a strong difference of opinion and putting it at the right level of risk assessment to make a final decision with the right information.

As part of the on-site evaluation, the agenda should be sent to the supplier with ample time for preparation. There are two positions when it comes to sending out the specifics to a supplier prior to an evaluation. One camp says not to send this out to them because it allows them to prepare ahead of time. But our position is that it will be a better outcome if you are transparent from the beginning of the relationship. Imagine being the person on the receiving end of your request—you would likely appreciate getting the information ahead of time so that you can be prepared. But be aware that having the information beforehand does not mean that issues won't be found. The ideal situation is that the supplier realizes the issue before the visit and takes the appropriate corrective action to address it. Again, you are making the final decision on the evaluation criteria, so the only bias is yourself. Part of the agenda that should be shared with the supplier is the list of questions that were identified as the relevant indicators in Table 4.2.

Table 4.1 TRF model with ranking and weighted values.

Attribute		Supplier A	Supplier B	Supplier C
Catheter development experience	Evaluate	1	1	1
	Weight value	1.5	1.5	1.5
	Risk	1.5	1.5	1.5
Robust process development	Evaluate	1	1	1
	Weight value	0.75	0.75	0.75
	Risk	0.75	0.75	0.75
Medium mix, HV Mfg capacity	Evaluate	1	1	1
	Weight value	1	1	1
	Risk	1	1	1
Regulatory experience	Evaluate	1	1	1
	Weight value	0.5	0.5	0.5
	Risk	0.5	0.5	0.5
Med device registered site	Evaluate	1	1	1
	Weight value	0.25	0.25	0.25
	Risk	0.75	0.25	0.25
TRF		4	4	4

Table 4.2 Relevant indicators.

What products can you show us that demonstrate your ability to develop catheter-based products?
Can you show us examples of the use of design for manufacturability? How do you assess products to this requirement?
Review of the site for these attributes
Who has been certified to the Regulatory Affairs Certification per RAPS? What specific certification? What products are registered with the FDA and what is the product number?
Review site ISO certification Review http://www.accessdata.fda.gov/scripts/cdrh/cfdocs/cfRL/rl.cfm for company registration (if the company is required to register with the FDA) and inspection results (e.g., 483, warning letters)
What type of engineering change control process is used? How are changes communicated to the supplier, and are there certain types of changes that don't require customer approval?

PRE-EVALUATION DISCUSSION WITH SUPPLIER

We are making the decision that we will give the supplier all the information ahead of the visit. Make sure the following are part of the visit agenda:

- Dates and times (schedule the visit within the facility's hours)
- Names and titles of individuals from your company

- Scope of the evaluation (ISO standards, FDA regulations, customer requirements)
- Any dietary/special considerations required
- Safety equipment requirements (steel toe shoes, safety glasses)
- Areas/processes to be reviewed
- Any questions that might be on the checklist or items to be reviewed during the site visit

Before the actual visit, we recommend that you call your contact to go over the agenda. This will not only help them be prepared but avoid any unnecessary issues before the visit. We've heard of instances where individuals made a lengthy trip to visit the supplier, only to be told upon arrival that they were not allowed to see any of the actual manufacturing areas. The audit had to be done from the conference room! If you learn that you will not be able to see the manufacturing area on an upcoming supplier visit, the issue should be addressed before the visit is made; if that is the supplier's final decision, then you have three options:

- Find another supplier
- Recommend a third-party assessment
- Conduct a desktop evaluation (have the supplier send you the documents and show them via a WebEx)

The good news is that you avoid the embarrassment of all involved when you show up and you can't accomplish the items on the agenda.

Again, it could be just the good military training that we had, but the idea is to "plan, plan, plan" so that when you have to make adjustments you'll be better prepared to accommodate them.

DESKTOP ASSESSMENT

> **Preamble to the 1996 QS Regulation, Comment #99**
>
> Where audits are not practical, this may be done through, among other means, reviewing historical data, monitoring and trending, and inspection and testing.

At one point, the distance between your company and a faraway supplier prevented you from conducting on-site assessments. However, with outsourcing becoming the norm for manufacturing, face-to-face interactions are key for successful business relationships. If the trip is cost prohibitive because of company financial constraints, consider using Skype or FaceTime to see your supplier's facility. "Go to the gemba!"

A desktop assessment may be considered when you are auditing a distributor that has multiple locations and you have additional controls that will be put in place for the products during incoming inspection or in process monitoring.

CONSULTANTS

For consultants, you can review their curriculum vitae (CV). Ensure during your review of the CV that the individual's background meets your needs. While John was working as a supplier quality engineer for a major IVD company, the CVs of two individuals who were to provide computer system validation consulting were submitted to him by the individuals' parent company for review. During his review, he discovered that one of the individuals did not meet the minimum requirements and could not perform the work for the company. The individual's CV did not contain any history/experience for the service John's company was seeking.

ON-SITE VISIT

The FDA understands that audits may not always be practical, but it still expects an assessment of the capability of the supplier to provide acceptable product or service. How this is done is dependent upon the product or service being provided. The most common methods used are inspection, testing, or review of a detailed statement of work (SOW) for the work completed.

Because of the resources involved in supplier audits, this should be considered for your major or critical suppliers that are associated with the risk of the product or service (contract manufacturer, calibration lab, sterilization, etc.) being provided.

Remember, you are the face of the customer to this new supplier. With any new relationship your first impressions are important as well as how you conduct yourself during your on-site visit. Maybe there was a time when a customer's auditor showed up who was less than professional or had a hidden agenda to fail your assessment. Going forward that impression is now associated with that customer, so make sure your impression is positive.

You should start the meeting by thanking the supplier for their time for your visit. After all the introductions are made, go over the agenda to make sure there aren't any questions or changes that have to be made (e.g., someone is out sick, activities going on in a certain area).

The approach that we have found to be the most effective regarding these types of evaluations is to use open-ended questions and the "show me" objective evidence approach. Using the questions and relevant indicators that were created during the planning phase, ask the supplier to explain how it meets these requirements. During these conversations, take notes and gather redacted examples to use for your report.

If time permits and the supplier is willing to provide the information, you may want to consider digging deeper into items such as:

- Technological capability
- Adequacy of manufacturing processes or equipment
- Adequate resources
- Experience/expertise
- Ability or willingness to adapt and respond to performance indicators

EXIT EVALUATION DISCUSSION WITH SUPPLIER

After the evaluation is complete, it's best to sit down and collect your thoughts in private before meeting with the supplier. The audit should not focus on just the nonconformances. If the supplier has some best practices it should be complimented on these, and you should ask whether you might be able to share them. As good quality auditors, we are taught to find three or four positive items that can be shared with the supplier as part of the exit interview.

As you outline your issues, it's best to group them together by topic or severity. From our experience, we recommend that you use the 3:2 rule—for every three compliments you identify only two issues. If this is the first time you've met these people or this company, you'll want to keep the relationship on a positive note. You can state that these are the major concerns, and any other items will be outlined in the report.

EVALUATING THE RESULTS

Now that you've completed your evaluations, you need to capture your assessment and evaluate it against those of the other potential suppliers. Using the example suppliers from Chapter 2, the TRF tool can be used to capture the comparison (see Table 4.3).

The criteria can be a simple checklist of items or a scale of 1–3:

1 = benchmarking processes

2 = compliant systems

3 = concerns of effectiveness/did not have this system

When we created this example, we purposely set some of the values to drive some of the questions:

- Just looking at the results, supplier B has the lowest TRF value overall, but . . .
  - Supplier B's manufacturing wasn't as good as that of the other suppliers
  - Supplier A didn't have the same development expertise that the other suppliers have, but its process development and manufacturing were excellent

Table 4.3 Comparison of suppliers using the TRF tool.

		Supplier		
Attribute		A	B	C
Catheter development experience	Evaluate	2	1	2
	Weight value	1.5	1.5	1.5
	Risk	3	1.5	3
Robust process development	Evaluate	1	1	2
	Weight value	0.75	0.75	0.75
	Risk	0.75	0.75	1.5
Medium mix, HV Mfg capacity	Evaluate	1	2	1
	Weight value	1	1	1
	Risk	1	2	1
Regulatory experience	Evaluate	2	1	2
	Weight value	0.5	0.5	0.5
	Risk	1	0.5	1
Med device registered site	Evaluate	3	1	1
	Weight value	0.25	0.25	0.25
	Risk	0.75	0.25	0.25
TRF		6.5	5	6.75

- Could supplier B develop the product and then transfer to supplier A with supplier C as a backup? Could you consider having them provide a first article, first lot, or prototypes to aid in assessing their ability to meet your requirements?
- Are there any other factors that you want to consider that weren't part of your initial factors, such as closeness to your facility or minority-owned status?

The answers should be part of the discussion the team has, but eventually one person has to make the final decision and the team needs to support it. Once the decision is made, the team should agree to see it through and stand behind it 100%.

DOCUMENTING YOUR DECISIONS

Now that doesn't mean something won't come up later and make you rethink your decision. The good news is that the information is documented and stored in the project file or some centralized documentation system. In the future, another project will come up and you can leverage the work that was already done.

At this point, the project leader should communicate with all the suppliers involved in this evaluation. The message should be concise and the decision process should be made clear.

The communication to the suppliers that weren't chosen should be done quickly and with sincere thanks for their time. As in most industries, these suppliers talk to each other, so how you handle this information is important to your company's reputation. We have seen suppliers that will not quote work from certain companies based on their experiences with those companies or rumors stated about those companies.

As we mentioned before, the FDA cannot review any of your supplier audits *under normal circumstances*:

> **5.6.2.2—Quality Audit**
>
> The inspectional approach for identifying inadequate auditing of a quality assurance program is limited by the agency's policy, which prohibits access to audit results. The policy is stated in CPG section 130.300 (7151.02). Under the QS/GMP regulation (21 CFR 820.180(c)) this prohibition extends to evaluations or audits of suppliers, 21 CFR 820.50(a), and Management Reviews conducted per 21 CFR 820.20. (US Food and Drug Administration 2015)

Therefore, we recommend that you have a cover letter for every audit that provides objective evidence that the QSRegs have been met. Here is a list that summarizes the following information:

- Supplier information
  - Name
  - Location
  - Contact
- Reason for approval
  - New
  - Status change/update
  - Disqualification

- Type of supplier
  - Product provider
  - Service provider
  - Consultant
- Rating
  - High
  - Medium
  - Low
  - Negligible
- Supplier history
- Supplier requirements
- Additional supplier requirements/controls
- Justification for supplier approval

If for some reason during your evaluation the supplier did not meet your minimum requirements, you will need to state your justification as to why you are still using the supplier. In addition to the justification you will need to define the type and extent of controls (see Chapter 5) to be exercised over your supplier to ensure the product conforms to your requirements.

We recommend that the approval contain at least two signatures: that of the individual recommending the supplier and that of the quality manager or their designee, or whatever your company's standard operating procedure (SOP) requires. Some companies also require individuals from the purchasing group to sign. Going beyond just a normal signature and date, you may want to indicate the intent of that individual's signature. For example:

> **Purchasing Manager or Designee**
>
> Your signature indicates that you have reviewed the requirements related to the purchasing process and any business risks associated with the supplier and that the risk is acceptable. Therefore, you approve the supplier for use by ABC Company.
>
> **Quality Manager or Designee**
>
> Your signature indicates that you have reviewed the requirements associated with the supplier and that applicable controls have been defined commensurate with the risk of the product being supplied. Therefore, you approve the supplier for use by ABC Company.

APPROVED SUPPLIER LIST (ASL)

FDA requirements of 21 CFR 820.50(a)(2)

(2) Define the type and extent of control to be exercised over the product, services, suppliers, contractors, and consultants, based on the evaluation results.

(3) Establish and maintain records of acceptable suppliers, contractors, and consultants.

What Is an ASL?

An ASL provides the first important level of supplier controls by specifying which suppliers have been approved to perform services for your company. The ASL is not a requirement of 21 CFR 820 and ISO 13485; however, the records of acceptable suppliers *are* required, thus making it an "industry norm" to manage your supplier base using the ASL tool.

This is important for the following reasons:

- Helps identify the level of controls based on the group and/or commodity of the service provided
- Identifies critical versus noncritical suppliers
- Keeps track of the approved suppliers versus the disqualified suppliers
- Helps the buyer place the purchase order with the appropriate suppliers
- Minimizes the variation in manufacturing by minimizing the number of inputs
- Helps scope out the amount of work that is required based on risk

The phrase "If everything is important, then nothing is important" applies to supplier management. Why would you require the same expectations of the office supply provider that you require of the precision machine parts or contract manufacturer? Defining the different types of commodities and associated risk allows the requirements to vary, which in turn makes good business and quality sense for risk prioritization and assigning resources.

From a purchasing point of view, the fewer purchase orders that need to be created and the fewer suppliers to manage, the better. Once a supplier has been established or approved, it's much easier to create what's called a blanket purchase order (larger quantity for usually a year period) and ask for releases against that one purchase order. It makes it much easier to set up replenishment systems such as kanbans. It's also easier to manage invoices since it's coming from the same supplier and purchase order.

From a quality perspective, this makes traceability of components through a kanban replenishment system much easier. Implemented correctly, each kanban shipment has a unique number, so if a quality issue occurs, tracking back to the shipment and manufacturing lot by the supplier is easier. If segregation of discrepant material is needed, the individual kanbans can be identified quickly.

From a manufacturing perspective, you want to minimize the variation on the input to your process. Otherwise, it makes it difficult to troubleshoot a problem within your own factory. You may create a control plan (to be discussed in Chapter 5) that is applicable to a specific supplier of a component or assembly. If the purchasing department places the order with another approved supplier, that same type of controls may not be applicable to that situation. Furthermore, you may have certain requirements that you've found only specific suppliers can meet. If that order goes to someone else, you may not end up with the same results.

At a minimum, the basics of the ASL should have date/revision control and should include these items (Table 4.4):

- Supplier name
- Supplier location (if multiple, list them all)
- Supplier number (unique value for each supplier)
- Approval status (approved, probation, disapproved)

The ASL should keep your company from using disqualified suppliers as well as control how new suppliers are added. This is not only for quality reasons but for business reasons as well. If your supply chain/purchasing team has negotiated special rates or pricing with a

Table 4.4 Example approved supplier list form.

Approved supplier list (June 8, 2015)			
Supplier name	Supplier location	Supplier number	Approval status

key supplier, then not using that supplier voids the work it's done. Also, there is a cost associated with adding another supplier that should be considered by the quality department. This includes the time to review and assess a new supplier, and the cost associated with a potential evaluation and the sustaining function.

Different Types of ASLs

- General approval—any supplier can be selected for any service (left up to the buyer to select the supplier)
- By commodity (machining, printed circuit boards, sheet metal, software services, contract manufacturing)
- By specific part number (part qualification for each supplier required)
- By category (risk based)

Depending on the type of manufacturing, device classification, risk assessment, and criticality of purchased items, the ASL can be set up in different approaches.

General Approval

Any supplier can be selected to provide the service. This could be commodities such as general office supplies (paper, pens, PCs, etc.), but make sure this is specific only to these situations. PCs used in manufacturing or with production equipment may not be applicable because of variables such as operating systems (Windows XP versus Windows 7) or different versions of software (Microsoft Excel). This is most applicable to Class I devices, in which the risk assessment is very low or the detection of variation is high (see Table 4.5).

By Commodity Grouping

Commodity grouping is the next level of controls that can be applied by different groupings of service (see Table 4.6).

> Again, simple is best, so it's up to the quality and purchasing departments to define levels that make sense and that can be implemented without creating a system that can't be managed. If you can make it just three levels, then use three levels; just make sure you clearly document it.

Examples of commodities include machining (small format), casting, welding, box-build/subassemblies, printed circuit board assemblies (PCBAs), printing, and sterilization. Note that each of these commodities can be broken up further if needed (e.g., EO versus gamma versus steam sterilization).

Table 4.5 Example approved supplier list form: general approval.

Approved supplier list (June 8, 2015)				
Supplier name	Supplier location	Supplier number	Approval status	Approval for these services

Table 4.6 Example approved supplier list form: by commodity.

Approved supplier list (June 8, 2015)				
Supplier name	Supplier location	Supplier number	Approval status	Commodity

By Specific Part Number

Depending on the criticality of the component, you may need to have the ASL broken down by specific part or item number. This should be reserved for the most critical items, the highest risk in your risk assessment, or special processes like coatings, sterilization, or software controls. If you need this level of controls, you may want to put something on the specific drawing or have it linked in your material requirements planning (MRP)/ordering system as an assurance that this occurs. Also, this may be listed in your quality plan for the development of your product (see Table 4.7).

Very few companies use the same ordering or MRP software; there are just too many out there to give you specific advice on how to annotate the specific items. However, all of these systems have an "Item Master" that contains specific attributes such as order quantity, make/buy, and primary supplier. We recommend you work with your purchasing and IT counterparts to determine the best method for implementation.

By Category

As mentioned in other chapters, we recommend creating your ASL with the identification of categories based on the risk associated with each supplier. These categories should help with the prioritization and risk assessment regarding sustaining activities such as PCPs and on-site audits (see Table 4.8).

Here are some definitions that you'll need to modify for your company in order to clarify these categories:

Critical (or high) supplier. A supplier of a product or service whose failure to meet specified requirements could cause unreasonable risk to the patient, clinician, or others as defined by your customers or could cause a significant degradation in product performance. A critical supplier is a supplier whose process is determined to be critical in nature to running the business. Critical suppliers will be designated on the ASL or in the site-specific procedure. Based on the risk level of the supplier and the assessment of the supply chain and quality team, the supplier may be designated as critical.

Table 4.7 Example approved supplier list form: by part number.

Approved supplier list (June 8, 2015)				
Supplier name	Supplier location	Supplier number	Approval status	Part number

Table 4.8 Example supplier category and risk rating.

Category	Risk level	Commodities
1	Critical or high	Contract manufacturers Outsourcing of software used in manufacturing
2	Medium	Precision components Printed circuit board assemblies
3	Low	Noncritical components Off-the-shelf items, noncritical
4	Negligible	Janitorial services Office supplies

Medium category. Those suppliers that provide bill-of-material or manufacturing-related materials, subassemblies, or fabricated custom product; or suppliers of processing or services whose performance could affect the ability of the products manufactured to conform to specifications. Some examples of level 1 suppliers whose performance mitigates the product's risk of nonconformance to the specification are suppliers of machined or molded parts and distributors of plastic polymers, assemblies, sterile unit packages, and coating and other treatments or processes, such as passivation or sterilization, which are used in the manufacture of finished products. This also includes any other suppliers whose failure to meet these quality performance requirements could have an adverse effect on product or process quality.

Low category. Those suppliers that provide services or materials that may come in contact with the finished device or whose goods or services could otherwise affect product quality. Examples of level 2 suppliers are consultants, calibration services, pest control services, shipping companies, distributors of manufactured chemicals, test labs, off-the-shelf distributors and/or suppliers of tooling (e.g., molds, jigs, and fixtures), and other processing and test equipment.

Negligible category. Those suppliers that provide non-manufacturing-related or non-quality-system-related products or services. Examples of suppliers are office supply, food service, and travel providers. These suppliers are not listed on the ASL but are entered into the financial/accounting system so that their services are paid for.

Each supplier should have one category, and if they could be in more than one, pick the higher value. If you need to customize some of your activities, you can always write a letter to file and rationalize your actions as needed (see Table 4.9).

Table 4.9 Example approved supplier list form: by category.

Approved supplier list (June 8, 2015)				
Supplier name	Supplier location	Supplier number	Approval status	Category

OTHER ITEMS TO CONSIDER

We want to remind you that anything you create has to be maintained. So don't add more information than what you can support with the resources you have. Before you automate your process, make sure you can do it well manually. Otherwise, you will automate a bad process.

These items may not be accessible to everyone else, nor made available during external inspection/audits, but they will help you make better decisions with the right information. Here is a list of items for your consideration:

- Last audit date
- Lead auditor name
- Quality agreement status
- Quality performance
- Delivery performance
- Late supplier corrective action requests
- Amount of money spent (same time period as the quality and delivery performance)—this one will come in handy later on when we discuss supplier consolidation efforts

The QSReg does not require an ASL, nor can the FDA investigator review supplier audit reports. However, the FDA can verify whether you are following your own procedures and whether you are showing compliance with 21 CFR 820.50 Purchasing Controls (see http://www.fda.gov/ICECI/Inspections/InspectionGuides/ucm114945.htm#9). You still need to make sure you are following your own procedures. For example, the following is an excerpt from a warning letter where the FDA cited a company for lack of adequate control when a supplier was disqualified for one product or service but not others. The supplier was left on the ASL for all products and services it provides, even though it performed poorly on another one and was disqualified for that product or service.

> Failure to define the type and extent of control to be exercised over the product, services, suppliers, contractors, and consultants, based on the evaluation results, as required by 21 CFR 820.50(a)(2). Specifically,
>
> Your supplier, which was used to fill ampoules, was disqualified for this service due to quality issues, but was left on your approved suppliers list because the supplier is still approved for other services. The supplier remained on the approved supplier list for all products and/or services. There is no method for disqualifying suppliers from providing specific products and/or services.

The procedure is only as good as the people who are using it and who understand what they need to do and can follow it every time.

Additionally, you may want to include on the supplier approval form a checklist that ensures you have all the documentation required by your local SOP. An example is provided on the CD accompanying this book.

SUMMARY/TAKEAWAY

- The evaluation work done in the previous chapters allows the evaluation of the suppliers to be conducted with flexibility and with data that will allow the best decision to be made. Using the TRF tool, the evaluation can be weighted to make sure the more important elements are identified.
- The TRF tool not only allows you to evaluate suppliers against the requirements but highlights the more weighted elements. When comparing suppliers we saw how invaluable that additional information was to make the best decisions.
- The TRF analysis can be documented and is easily defendable in front of any external agency or customer.
- The ASL can be created and maintained in many different ways, but you should pick the method that can be best sustained by your organization.

WHAT'S NEXT?

- Implementing a mix of controls at your supplier and in-house to ensure products and services meet your requirements. We will discuss these controls in the next chapter.

5

Controls: Are They Still Meeting Our Needs?

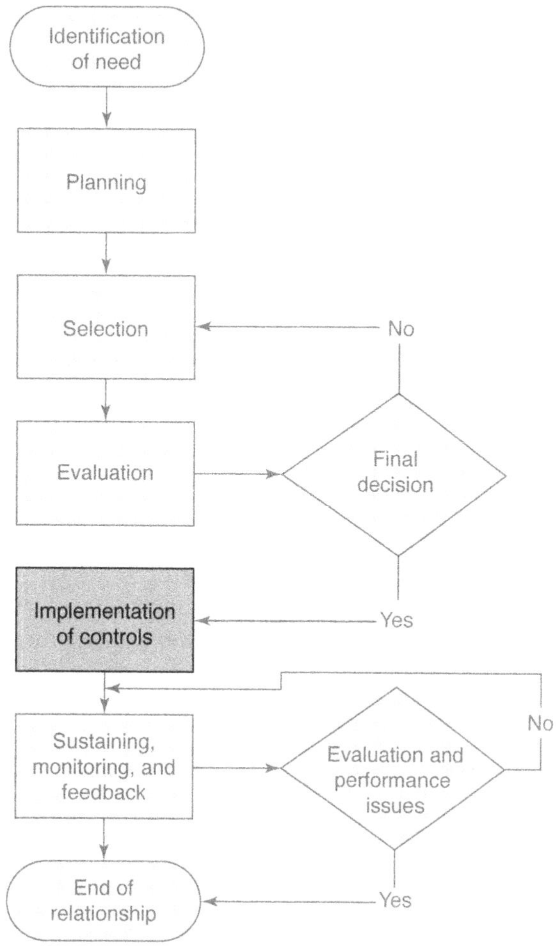

MAIN TAKEAWAYS FROM THIS CHAPTER

- We cover how to look at the product design and use it to determine the initial controls. Once those controls are in place, the next logical place to look is at the process and then link the controls with the process to create the process control plan.
- Implementing controls at your facility through receiving inspection activities can be done in different ways, from incoming inspection to process control plans and process audits.

- The cost of quality should be a good tool to measure where the controls have been implemented, as well as a potential leverage for risk and cost reductions.
- Creating the strategic supplier map will help with making decisions on risk mitigation and the intent of pushing the right controls to the closest point possible—at the supplier.
- We cover how good supplier controls and change controls are communicated and verified.

The FDA requires the device manufacturer to have in place controls based on the results of the evaluation per 21 CFR 820.50(a)(2):

> Define the type and extent of control to be exercised over the product, services, suppliers, contractors, and consultants, based on the evaluation results.

ISO 13485:2016 does not explicitly state the same thing as the FDA regulation, but it's implied by making a statement about monitoring and reevaluation of your suppliers. We feel the type of monitoring you impose on your supplier will be based on the results of the evaluation as stated in 21 CFR 820.50(a)(2). The changes in ISO 9001:2015 subclause 8.4.2 Type and extent of control are more in line with the FDA's requirement.

We believe that using Juran's strategic view with your suppliers makes for a better relationship for all parties involved with the main focus being the safety of the end user. Relationships that are built on communication and trust help in understanding the expectations and in fulfilling them. The best way to demonstrate these characteristics is through process controls.

In this chapter we will touch on various controls you may impose on your suppliers based on the results of the evaluation. The controls we mention are not all-inclusive but can help you reach into your toolbox and pick the right one for the given situation. The requirement, regardless of the type of device and supplier, is that the manufacturer must have some form of control over its suppliers based on the results of the evaluation, risk, and some documented rationale. That doesn't mean that the same controls are imposed on the supplier of critical machined parts and on the supplier of office supplies. However, it does mean you need to specify the requirements and document the expectation.

As always, the preamble is a good source of information. Here is the FDA's thinking on supplier controls, taken from comment #99 of the preamble:

> A finished device manufacturer may choose to provide greater in-house controls to ensure that products and service meet requirements, or may require the supplier to adopt measures necessary to ensure acceptability, as appropriate. FDA generally believes that an appropriate mix of supplier and manufacturer quality controls are necessary.

Why do you need to look at these controls? There are expectations that are required per 21 CFR 820, ISO 13485, and other regulatory requirements. Then, there are just good business practices that you should incorporate that will also keep external auditors satisfied during their assessments of your company. If you remember from the earlier chapters, inadequate supplier controls shows up on 40% of the warning letters issued by the FDA. If you look at your own company's performance, it may show up in high inspection costs or internal costs.

Because we feel that supplier quality agreements (SQAs) are a vital means of laying out controls with suppliers (critical and some major suppliers), and because we have seen increased scrutiny from the review of FDA warning letters, we have devoted a full chapter to

SQAs. Therefore, in this chapter we will just mention that the SQA is one means of relaying the needed controls to your suppliers.

Although there are many controls that you could impose on your suppliers, we will focus on a few primary controls used most often. We will show how the strategic supplier map can be implemented—starting from incoming inspection of product, through process validation and into control plans, and finally to change management.

TYPES OF CONTROLS

How Do Risk Management and Design Controls Link to Supplier Controls?

This is not a deep dive into risk management but a very high-level overview of the various levels of controls you might impose on your suppliers based on the results of the evaluation.

When we think of different controls we can put in place, we are somewhat fooled by the number of controls and think we have a multitude to pick from. The bottom line is that there are really only three levels that various methods fit under. You may not realize this, but at some point in time you have encountered one or all three levels when crossing railroad tracks. The three levels of controls are:

- Information only
- Physical barriers
- Designing out the risk

Information Only

In Figure 5.1 we have our least desirable control, which is "information only," or warnings. These controls are found on product warning labels, in the information for use provided with the product, and through product knowledge given to care providers. We have signs/

Figure 5.1 Control by labeling only.

warnings, but there is nothing preventing us from bypassing this level of control. We decide when it's safe enough to cross when a train is approaching. This is much like telling your supplier to make sure it makes the product to the specification before shipping it to the customer. We are allowing the supplier to make the decision for us without preventing it from bypassing our requirements.

Physical Barriers

In Figure 5.2 there is a physical barrier (arm/guard) that comes down when the train approaches the crossing.

At some point someone decided that when the train is x distance away from the railroad crossing, it will trigger a switch that in turn lowers the arm to prevent people from crossing the tracks. This level of control, most commonly used and in most cases preventing us from bypassing the control, is a physical barrier. For example, the design of a certain therapy device will work if the disposable part is correctly connected to the power device, or the two mating devices won't work until they are aligned correctly, which completes the circuit.

With this type of control, we are implementing protective measures such as guards, alarms, or inspections utilized on the device or in the manufacturing process. We may require our supplier to conduct process capability analysis or use statistical process control (SPC) when manufacturing our product.

This type of control is not completely mistake proof, but it prevents the majority of mistakes from bypassing the control. However, even when warnings or physical barriers are in place, they are not completely foolproof. Figure 5.3 shows what can happen in instances where the warnings or physical barriers are ignored.

Unfortunately, this is where a patient may be injured. The patient could burn their body due to improper grounding of a device or, worse, they might not survive the procedure.

Designing out the Risk

The best form of control is to design out the risk completely. It's very rare when we deal with suppliers or even internally that we completely design the risk out of the product or manufacturing process. Sometimes when we design out one risk we inadvertently introduce another risk.

Figure 5.2 Control by physical barrier.

Figure 5.3 Result of ignoring controls.

Figure 5.4 Control by designing out the risk.

As displayed in Figure 5.4, the railroad tracks cross above the road, preventing a potential collision. However, by designing out the risk of a potential collision, we may have introduced the risk of a vehicle passing under the bridge being too tall and crashing into the bridge. Of course, if that were the case the process would need to start all over.

Could the road be excavated to allow for larger trucks? Could early signals/indicators be put in place to stop these larger trucks from getting too close to these bridges? Could their GPS devices be programmed to take them around these potential hazards? It comes down to the risk/benefit/cost ratio that has to be decided.

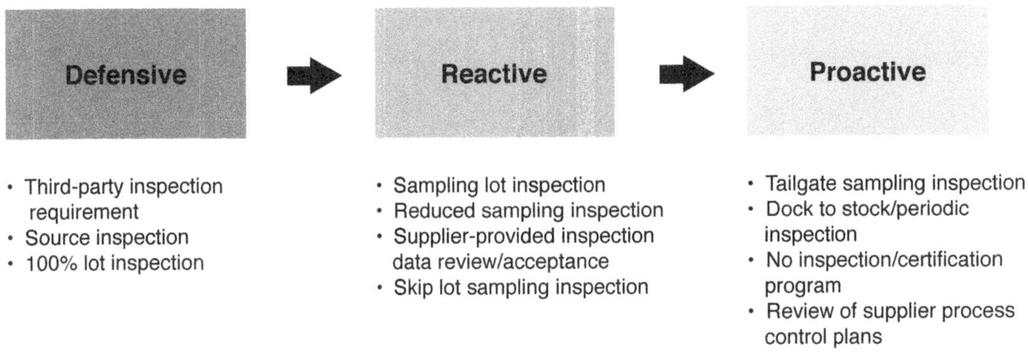

Figure 5.5 Strategic supplier map.

STRATEGIC SUPPLIER MAP: BEGIN WITH THE END IN MIND

As with any strategic planning exercise, it is best to know where you want to end up and chart your course accordingly. Be it getting between Hyannis, Massachusetts, and Martha's Vineyard on a 30-foot boat or putting together your company's strategic business plan, both start with identifying your current position and where you want to go. The time duration and resource consideration have to be part of this strategy, but without knowing them, you could run out of both before you reach your destination. A map will help keep you on course even when you hit some unexpected weather. Proper planning keeps you from running out of resources (or gas) before reaching your destination.

In order to get started, it's best to give some consideration to the strategic supplier map (see Figure 5.5). This road map gives you a high-level look at how current controls are categorized from a perspective of risk and effectiveness. As quality professionals, we are always asked to do more with less, and this map will help you determine the most cost-effective decision. For those who already have a system in place, this might help you look at your current system and perform a gap assessment to identify areas for improvement. For those who already have a robust process, this may help you do some benchmarking against other companies.

HOW TO IMPLEMENT THE STRATEGIC SUPPLIER MAP

The idea of this road map is to move supplier controls to the closest possible point of detection once you have gained confidence with your supplier—starting from incoming inspection of product, through process validation and into control plans, and finally to change management.

USING THE SIPOC METHOD TO IMPLEMENT THE STRATEGIC SUPPLIER MAP

We have used one of the more powerful improvement tools to help create the strategic supplier map. SIPOC stands for supplier, input, process, output, and customer. The SIPOC tool is very effective to help understand the current process so that improvements can be made, as well as to help visually describe the future process (see Figure 5.6).

In order to get going on the map, you need to do the following:

1. Identify product/process with the highest risk
2. Determine what controls are needed for these critical items

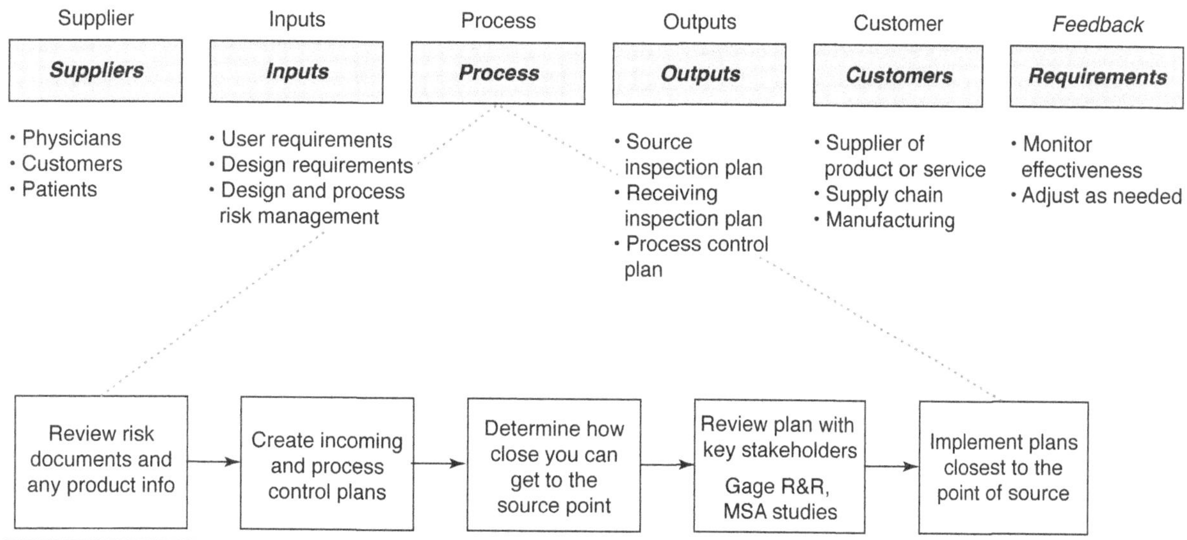

Figure 5.6 Strategic supplier map—SIPOC diagram.

3. Determine the cost/benefit of the controls
4. Implement the right controls at your company and at the supplier
5. Determine where you would like to be in your value/cost proposition and by when

These items may not be all-inclusive for your situation, but they are a good start for implementing your strategic supplier map.

First Things First: What Is the Product Risk?

As we mentioned earlier in this chapter, the first thing that needs to be identified is the product risk based on critical-to-quality (CTQ) characteristics. In order to determine the risk category, you may need to return to the discussion of TRF in Chapter 3 and use that information in this disposition.

Using the risk analysis and mitigation tools that were used in the design controls element should be a great starting point to determine the appropriate controls. If you are a subcontractor to the actual product design owner, these controls may be identified on the drawing/specifications as CTQ characteristics. If they are not clear, then the best thing to do is ask.

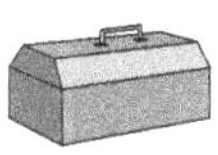

If you are truly in a partnership, your customer will provide you with the information. Some of the best practices that we've seen in quality are part of the contract review process. The cross-functional team led by the sales team would have a daily standing meeting to review these quotations. Their job was to identify the quality-specific elements that were outside the current capabilities, identify tolerances that might be an issue controlling within their current capabilities, and identify any CTQ characteristics that might be missing. The amount of time that this requires is quickly offset by avoiding upsetting a customer when a quality issue occurs. Contract review is not just an ISO requirement.

It is understood that the effort and cost will most likely be higher for those products with a higher risk profile. Therefore, the recommended approach is to focus on the critical few, not the trivial many.

Table 5.1 lists the four categories that can be applied to the actual items produced by these suppliers and the associated risk value.

A good exercise is to take the bill of materials for a product that is currently in production and see if you can assign the category for each item. Count up the number of items and compare them with Table 5.2. The percent you calculate may be different than what is shown in this table. Most likely you will determine that the majority of work will focus on the critical and high-risk items. We recommend you work on these items first based on the risk category.

Table 5.1 Design FMEA table.

Effect	Criteria: Severity of effect	Ranking
Hazardous	Very high severity ranking when a potential failure mode affects safe product operation. Noncompliance with government regulations. Patient death.	10
High	Product inoperable, with loss of primary function. Customer very dissatisfied.	8
Moderate	Product operable, but nonessential system inoperable. Customer experiences discomfort or dissatisfaction.	6
Low	Fit and finish does not conform. Defect noticed by most customers.	4
Minor to none	Fit and finish does not conform. Defect noticed by discriminating (<25%) customers, or no effect	2

Table 5.2 Risk category and estimated percent of your product.

Category	Definition	Estimated percentage of your product*
Critical	A subset of high risk, these are items that would certainly cause patient harm/death if a failure occurred If the supplier did not deliver the product, the shipment of finished product would be greatly impacted	5%
High risk	Process to deliver parts is probably very complex Materials required may be difficult to process Specifications dictate complex test requirements Parts may be single sourced	45%
Medium	Process to deliver the part is moderately complex Parts can be sourced from several suppliers with the correct skills/expertise Technology is understood and common in industry	40%
Low	Process to make the parts is simple with little chance for error Materials are readily available and simple to process	10%

*Estimate is based on our experience from previous companies but may not reflect your business model. However, it is important to remember the old adage "If everything is a priority, then nothing is a priority." The same applies here: figure out what is the biggest risk based on these categories and work on the highest values first.

Determine What Controls Are Needed for These Critical Items

Level of controls based on risk and results of the supplier evaluation—this is a list from the most stringent to the most ideal levels that can be used to implement controls (see Table 5.3):

- Third-party inspection requirement
- Source inspection
- 100% lot inspection
- Sampling lot inspection
- Reduced sampling inspection
- Supplier-provided inspection data review/acceptance
- Skip lot sampling inspection
- Tailgate sampling inspection
- Dock to stock/periodic inspection
- No inspection/certification program
- Review of supplier process control plans

The correct controls will be based on several factors, but one of the most important factors is the risk to the patient if the component or product fails. You may want to know the following: How mature is the supplier's quality system? How well did it meet your requirements during your evaluation? These and other questions should be asked of each and every supplier so you can have in place the correct controls for the given situation.

Table 5.3 Control factors: cost and resources.

Control	Cost	Resources
Third-party inspection requirement	High	Third-party inspectors
Source inspection	High	Traveling inspectors
100% lot inspection	High	In-house inspection and required metrology equipment
Sampling lot inspection	Medium	In-house inspection and required metrology equipment
Reduced sampling inspection	Medium	In-house inspection and required metrology equipment
Supplier-provided inspection data review/acceptance	Medium	In-house inspection and less metrology equipment
Skip lot sampling inspection	Low	In-house inspection and less metrology equipment (less frequent)
Tailgate sampling inspection	Low	In-house inspection and less metrology equipment (less frequent)
Dock to stock/periodic inspection	Low	In-house inspection and less metrology equipment (less frequent)
No inspection/certification program	Ideal	In-house inspectors/traveling inspectors Little to no required metrology equipment
Review of supplier process control plans	Ideal	Traveling engineers and inspectors based on performance (not schedule)

We do not recommend having a "one size fits all" approach. However, we do recommend using supplier categories to identify the best controls for that grouping of suppliers. You can always modify them based on outliers or other circumstances, but keeping it simple is the key to effective execution.

Once you figure out what controls can be used, based on either individual suppliers or categories of suppliers, then you can figure out the "TO BE" situation.

Implement the Right Controls at Your Company and at the Supplier

After reviewing your "AS IS" state, you may realize that your costs and resources are not sustainable. Also, you may see that the same resource group could be more useful by being proactive and conducting supplier assessments rather than performing incoming inspection. Either way, you'll want to figure out how to move the "true inspection" closest to the source of detection—the process at the supplier.

This may appear to be advocating for removal of incoming inspection altogether, and that would be a true statement. The defensive position of trying to review quality is a huge cost of quality. There are research studies that show product quality is not affected by the increase of incoming inspection levels (Devine 2009). However, to be fair, there is value in having incoming inspection in place during the beginning of the process, which will be explained within the next couple of pages.

Source Inspection

Source inspection may be the best method for large, complicated parts for which you may not have the equipment for performing the inspection or the room for staging the parts. This inspection method gets you very close to the supplier, which allows you to meet the people involved and see the operations at the same time. The other benefit of this method is that if there is an issue, your inspector can call back to the engineering group to discuss the issue and provide information that might not be as easily communicated by the supplier. Also, this type of inspection may be best for inspecting large lots of material that are accepted at one time and shipped over time.

It's expected that the control plans for the supplier have been provided ahead of time. In some cases, the plans may be the critical features identified on the drawing or specification. The preferred method is that the control plan is created by you and the supplier and identifies the critical features, the controls to be used, and the sampling plan/frequency. More information regarding control plans will be outlined later in this chapter, but we highly recommend creating the control plan early on in the development process. This is where engineering and operations must be involved.

Before establishing this requirement at the supplier, make sure you have some internal procedures that document how you will handle the following:

- Accepted product—Do you need paperwork or a sticker that would be put on the parts? This would signify that the parts were accepted and, upon receipt at your company, could be put directly into the point of use.
- Rejections—How are you going to document these issues? How are you going to keep track of past issues? Is this going to be used to track supplier performance?
- Reworking and repairing issues—What is your policy on these two types of activities? Do you have time to allow for the reworking of parts? If the parts require reworking, are there any outside processes that will cause further delay? If the parts require repair, who at your company must approve them first?

We recommend that you first figure out these questions. Our recommendations follow:

- Accepted product—For paperwork, use the same method you use for accepting parts internally; just have a way of identifying that the inspection was a source inspection versus an incoming inspection. Most companies that we've worked with have some form of inspection folder that contains the inspection history by item. Many companies have made these records electronic, so you may have to download/print specific files before you conduct the inspection.
- Identification of product—Create labels with specific information that will allow the receiver at your company to know that these parts were accepted.
  - The label should go on the container closest to the parts without damaging the actual product. For example, if the parts are put in a plastic bag, and that is how the parts are stored in your inventory location, then the label would go on that bag. If the parts are so large that they come inside a separate box, then the label would go on the outside of that container.
  - Each label should have a space for the inspector to initial and date. This allows for traceability of acceptance in case of an issue.
  - If there are multiple items being shipped, you should consider a spot on the label to identify how many labels were provided in this specific source inspection (e.g., 1 of 30). This also provides confirmation that all the items that were accepted did in fact get shipped and didn't get lost during shipment.
  - To avoid any confusion, provide only the number of labels needed based on the product that is being source inspected. This avoids any mislabeling of accepted product.
- Rejections—Before writing up any paperwork, review the specifics with the supplier to make sure it confirms. Consider using a "hold" form that places the product on hold until a second person can verify the issue before making it a noncompliance. If there's a measurement issue, it would be best to document the issue so when it is corrected, there is a record to show what was done. It doesn't mean you have to issue a corrective action request, and the supplier will appreciate that additional work isn't created. Also, this strengthens the relationship with your supplier by treating them respectfully. Once the issue is confirmed, you may use the same method that you would follow if the inspection were done in your facility.
  - This may not be possible because of the MRP transaction that would be done or because the nonconforming material databases aren't accessible outside your company. Therefore, it's best to create a method to capture these issues for traceability and performance reasons. If you cannot stay for the reworking of the parts, the next inspector will know what happened and where you left off.
  - The actual information should be entered into your system that is used for tracking these nonconforming issues, especially for performance tracking. We have seen systems that don't include source inspection when supplier performance calculations are done, and the data look only at incoming material. For data integrity and the purpose of normalizing data, it's important to include these rejections in your analysis.
- Reworking and repairing—Review and agree upon definitions regarding rework and repair. Here are some general definitions and examples:
  - Rework: The act of reprocessing noncomplying product, through the use of original or alternate equivalent processing, in a manner that ensures compliance of the product with applicable drawings or specifications. Example: tire pressure is low and air is added to bring it back up to the right pressure.

- Repair: Action on a nonconforming product to make it conform to requirements. Unlike rework, repair can affect or change parts of the nonconforming product. Example: tire pressure is low and a hole is found in the tire. A patch is applied and air is added to bring the tire back up to the right pressure (the product will most likely work but it has been changed).

Once the supplier informs you that the material is ready for inspection, you should plan to go there as quickly as possible (some pre-planning as well as a contingency plan might be needed). Ask the supplier to have these items ready for you upon your arrival:

- Purchase order
- Specification, drawings, and any relevant documents (e.g., material certs, Certificate of Compliance)
- Inspection results (results documented per the control plan)
- All the parts staged in the inspection area
- All the required inspection tools

Be sure to ask whether you will need to bring safety shoes, ear protection, or safety glasses.

Go through all the paperwork and verify that the inspection results meet the specifications, drawing requirements, and control plan. If you don't have the control plan, use the inspection methods you would have used if the parts hadn't been source inspected. This will give you insight on how effective this plan would have been if the parts had been inspected at your facility.

Also, during this time you may ask to review previous corrective actions and see the implementation of the actions and their effectiveness. These may come from previous audits or nonconformances that were identified at your facility.

Remember, you are the ambassador of your company and sometimes the only person that the supplier will meet from your company. The supplier's perceptions of your company come from your visits, so be respectful at all times. This doesn't mean you have to compromise on quality or be willing to ignore problems.

As discussed earlier, this review of the material at the supplier allows you to gain confidence in its quality systems. As you identify suppliers and material that can be accepted by reviewing their inspection data (supplier data review), these are easy candidates for this process, which can save money and time for both you and the supplier.

Incoming Inspection

The traditional method of inspection is performing incoming inspection at your facility. Though it's not the most proactive method, it is the best method if done correctly—based on risk.

Most companies use a default acceptance quality limit, which is not based on risk assessment, but instead should focus on the failure modes and effects analysis (FMEA) created during the design controls of the actual product. The other mistake is to base the sample size for attribute inspection plans on variable sampling plans, which are not the same quantity.

The main difference in taking the samples is that for a variable sample, measurements of a continuous characteristic of interest are taken, with a mean and standard deviation calculated; for an attribute sample, one counts the number of units having or not having specific properties (mostly good/bad or number of flaws). Generally, attribute sampling plans are much larger than variable sampling plans, and to be useful, they need to be very large when the proportion of bad units (or flaws) is very small. However, the main benefit of using variable data is that a variable sampling plan requires a much smaller sample size than an attribute sampling plan.

The bottom line is that percent defective (LTPD) may be one value but the sampling plan sizes are not the same, so use the right one for the right application.

Limiting Quality versus Acceptance Quality Limit for Inspection

We recommend the limiting quality (LQ) approach for incoming inspection as opposed to the acceptance quality limit (AQL) approach.

Before we get into the specifics, we offer a list of definitions of terms that will be covered. It should be noted that this is not a complete course in statistics; we just cover some very basic concepts. If you are not comfortable with statistics, we highly recommend you reach out to a statistical consultant or seek additional training on the use of statistics.

- AQL—the acceptance quality limit is the quality level that is the worst tolerable process average when a continuing series of lots is submitted for acceptance sampling.
- LQ—the limiting quality is when a lot is considered in isolation, a quality level that, for the purposes of sampling inspection, is limited to a low probability of acceptance. Also known as lot tolerance percent defective.
- LTPD—the lot tolerance percent defective is the level of quality that is unsatisfactory and therefore should be rejected by the sampling plan. A consumer's risk of 0.10 is common, and LTPD has been defined as the lot quality for which the probability of acceptance is 0.10, that is, 10% of such lots will be accepted.
- Operating characteristic (OC) curve—a graphical display of the fraction nonconforming versus the probability of accepting the lot.
- α = producer's risk, which is the risk of a manufacturer rejecting conforming product (also called Type I error)—AQL holds α constant and protects the producer.
- β = consumer's risk, which is the risk of the manufacturer accepting nonconforming product (also called Type II error)—LQ holds β constant and protects the consumer.
- Nonconforming classification
  - *Critical:* Classification that experience or judgment indicates is likely to cause unsafe conditions for those who use, maintain, or depend on the product or is likely to prevent performance of the end item function. Example: package sterility is jeopardized.
  - *Major:* Classification other than critical that may cause the product to fail, cause poor performance, shorten product life, or prevent interchangeability. Example: the torque rate is higher than the allowable spec.
  - *Minor:* Not likely to materially reduce the usability of the unit. Example: pump housing has scratches.

Here's some background on inspection plans:

- Per ANSI/ASQ Z1.4-2003 (p. 65) the concept of AQL only applies when an acceptance sampling scheme with rules for switching between normal, tightened, and reduced inspection and discontinuance of sample inspections is used.
- In addition, ANSI/ASQ Z1.4-2003 states the AQL alone does not describe the protection to the consumer for individual lots or batches, but is more directly related to what is expected from a series of lots or batches provided the provisions of this standard are satisfied. See first bullet point.
- When lots are considered isolated (validations), infrequent, small, or "special" (again, validations), a sampling plan that is indexed on the consumer's risk should be utilized (i.e., LQ).

To determine the capability of a new process to produce a good product, a sampling plan based on LTPD should be used. Then we can state after successful completion of the validation that we are either 95% or 99% confident that not more than $LTPD_{p\%}$ is defective. The industry standard is typically 95% confidence. If the process step is very critical, we can increase the confidence to 99%. This will drive our sample size up as well as ensure that our process is capable at the stated confidence and content as long as we are below the allowable nonconforming acceptance number.

Table 5.4 lists several sampling plans using 95% confidence with an associated upper nonconforming limit. Other confidence limits may be chosen, but these are not displayed in the table.

As an example of how to read Table 5.4, say you are determining the capability of your cassette labeling process to ensure the label is placed right side up. You pick a defect rate of 5% since a label will be placed on the cassette regardless of orientation (more of a cosmetic issue when placed upside down). By selecting Ac = 0 defects, your sample size n = 60, regardless of lot size (based on the binomial distribution) under the assumption of a significantly large lot size. If all 60 cassettes are inspected with 0 nonconforming, you can state with 95% confidence that your percent defective is not greater than 5%. If you find 1 nonconforming, you cannot state this claim.

You cannot say "I will look at another 35 to take me to 95" since you found one reject. This is a common mistake and is not how the sampling plan works. You would state your acceptance as $c = 1$, then your sample size would be 95. This offers the same protection as the first example and so on for $c = 2$.

Let us provide some basic explanation regarding AQL, LTPD, and the OC curve (refer to Figure 5.7). The probability of acceptance and percent defective make up the vertical and horizontal axes, respectively. The AQL represents a level of defects routinely accepted by the sampling plan. Based on the intersection of that point on the OC curve, you can determine the probability of acceptance.

Whenever a sampling plan rejects a lot, one can state with 95% confidence that the lot is above the AQL. This is a result of the fact that lots at or below the AQL are not likely to be rejected. The level of confidence, 95%, is a direct result of the fact that at the AQL there is a 95% chance of acceptance.

The $LTPD_{0.10}$ is defined to be that percent defective with a 10% chance of acceptance. Figure 5.7 shows that for the single sampling plan n = 50 and a = 1, the $LTPD_{0.10}$ is 7.56% defective. The $LTPD_{0.10}$ represents a level of defects routinely rejected by the sampling plan.

Whenever a sampling plan accepts a lot, one can state with 90% confidence that the lot is below the $LTPD_{0.10}$. This is a result of the fact that lots at or above the $LTPD_{0.10}$ are not likely to be accepted. The level of confidence, 90%, is equal to 100% – 10%, where 10% is the chance of acceptance at the $LTPD_{0.10}$.

The AQL and $LTPD_{0.10}$ represent special cases of percentiles of the OC curve. The AQL is the 95th percentile, while the $LTPD_{0.10}$ is the 10th percentile. Other percentiles can be used as

Table 5.4 LTPD based on a 95% confidence interval.

Confidence	Upper limit	Ac = 0	AQL	Ac = 1	AQL	Ac = 2	AQL
95%	5%	n = 60	.08%	n = 95	.41%	n = 155	.54%
95%	2.5%	n = 120	.04%	n = 190	.22%	n = 310	.33%
95%	1%	n = 300	.02%	n = 470	.08%	n = 630	.13%

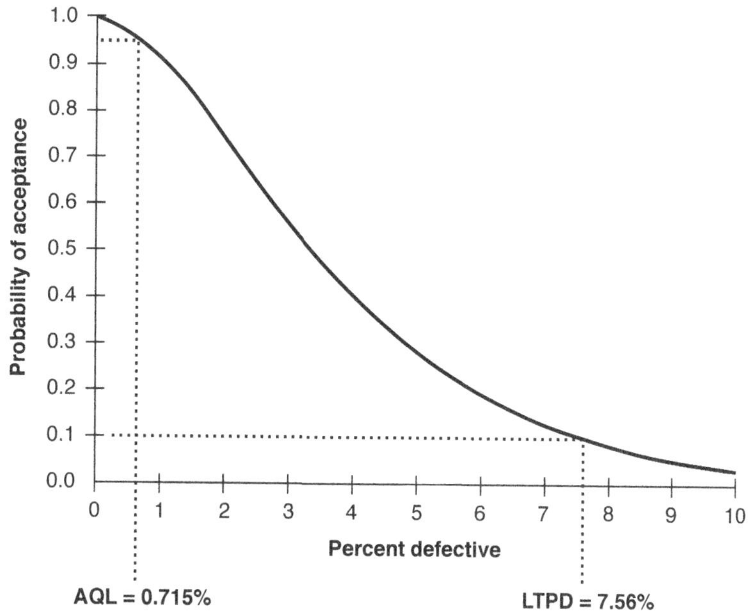

Figure 5.7 OC curve of a single sampling plan.

Source: Taylor Enterprises, http://www.variation.com/techlib/as-6.html.

well. The $LTPD_{0.05}$ is the fifth percentile. If a lot is accepted, one can state with 95% confidence that the lot is below the $LTPD_{0.05}$.

Summary

- AQL is applicable to continuous manufacturing with switching rules applied
- LQ is used for isolated or special lots, which is more suited to validation
- AQL has a high probability of acceptance when the process average is at or below the AQL
- LQ has a low probability of acceptance when the lot is at or above the percent defective
- Use of LQ allows your company to take a more risk-based approach to sample size selection as opposed to lot size determining the sample size
- AQL protects the producer by not rejecting a potentially good lot
- LQ protects the consumer by not accepting a potentially bad lot

OK, How Do I Get Started with Sampling Plans?

First, go online and buy the applicable standards so you have a reference copy. Go over the documents and understand the differences between the two approaches. Try searching on the internet and you'll find plenty of resources that explain this information.

Don't default to the "standard 1% AQL" for everything. As an example, Table 5.5 lists valid attribute sample sizes for specified confidence and reliability expectations with no defects allowed (LTPD). The inspection control plan that is created for each item (or for groups of similar commodities) can state the specifics based on the associated risk.

You might have noticed that the quantity of samples for attribute data is much larger than that for variable data (another good reason to focus on variable data inspection plans). Again, this is based on LTPD, which should tie back to the product risk (Tables 5.6 and 5.7).

Table 5.5 Attribute sample sizes based on confidence and reliability levels.

	Sample size (n) when $d = 0$ (or Acc = 0, Rej = 1)								
Confidence (%)	90 (Low risk)			95 (Medium risk)			99 (High risk)		
Reliability (%)	90	95	99	90	95	99	90	95	99
Sample size (n)	22	28	230	45	60	299	230	300	459

Table 5.6 Attribute testing.

Attribute testing (Acc = 0, Rej = 1)			
	LTPD		
Lot size	**5%**	**10%**	**15%**
0 to 50	26	18	11
51 to 100	36	20	13
101 to 200	40	21	14
201 to 300	41	21	14
301 to 600	43	22	14
601 to 3000	44	22	14
3001 and up	45	22	14

Variable testing			
		Minimum accept criteria	
LTPD	**Sample size**	**1-sided**	**2-sided**
15%	15	Ppk = 0.58	Ppk = 0.60, Pp = 0.67
10%	15	Ppk = 0.69	Ppk = 0.70, Pp = 0.76
5%	15	Ppk = 0.86	Ppk = 0.86, Pp = 0.90

Table 5.7 Risk category definitions.

Risk category	Definition
High risk	Process to deliver parts is probably very complex Materials required may be difficult to process Specifications dictate complex test requirements Parts may be single sourced
Medium risk	Process to deliver the part is moderately complex Parts can be sourced from several suppliers with the correct skills/expertise Technology is understood and common in industry
Low risk	Process to make the parts is simple with little chance for error Materials are readily available and simple to process

Based on the risk level identified for each item, you may use the different LTPD percent. So for high-risk parts you may select 5% LTPD while low-risk parts may use 15%. As you can see from the tables, the sample size is based on the total quantity of the lot, which will vary based on your receipts. If the supplier has shipped in three separate receipts from the same lot, you may document that you are taking your samples equally from all three lots to determine the acceptance (and rejection). Just don't forget to document your rationale for doing so and the outcome!

Supplier Data Review

The next step after getting your incoming inspection process in place is to look at the potential of accepting product based on supplier data. We say this is the next step in the process because if this product was originally accepted at source inspection and then moved to incoming inspection, then this is the next step of leveraging the supplier controls. When you think about it, you've already paid the supplier to make the product per a specification or drawing, so why can't you rely on its inspection data?

This method is more common in other industries but has started to become a standard practice in the medical device industry.

In order to put this in place, some things have to be done first:

- Get agreement from the supplier that it will provide this information with every shipment. The best place to document this requirement is in the purchase specification.
- Conduct some sort of gage/measurement verification with the supplier so the results are within acceptable limits.
- Get agreement from the supplier that it will keep these records based on the record retention period stated in the supplier quality agreement or terms on the purchase order.
- There is some incentive for the supplier to put this process in place. For example, part performance will be weighed against the decision for annual audits. This is a great example of supplier controls with low cost and a benefit to everyone.
- There is an incentive to you as the customer because this helps you identify candidates for skip lot inspection, reduced inspection, and process control plans. We haven't compromised quality while moving toward the most effective place to put these controls—at the supplier.

To help gain acceptance by the supplier, we offer this talking point: there is some incentive for the supplier to put this process in place. For example, part performance will be weighed against the decision for annual audits. This is a great example of supplier controls with low cost and a benefit to everyone.

What Should Be Part of the Supplier Data Review Document?

There are many versions of the supplier data review document, and the basic items that need to be included are as follows:

- Part number and revision
- Specification number and revision (if different from part number and revision)
- Critical dimension/specification
- Sampling plan
- Description of inspection method (list primary and alternates if applicable)
- Inspection equipment used (list primary and alternates if applicable)
- Reaction plan (if out-of-tolerance conditions are encountered)

Please remember this document for later discussions of process control plans in this chapter. The format is very similar and this will make the transition for both the supplier and you much easier.

Once you've identified the supplier and components, you may want to have a trial period where you can verify the measurements and the documents. The trial period may vary based on risk, but during this period you shouldn't have any rejections. Also, you don't want to keep these items in the program if any rejections are found later on in the process that are determined to be the supplier's responsibility. You may want to consider any supplier audit findings to see whether there is any impact on the items within the program.

Remember the old adage "If it wasn't documented, then it didn't happen." During this program, there may be situations where assignable causes can be identified that should be considered in the decision-making process to keep an item in the program. However, since the decision wasn't well documented or stored with the actual records, you will have inadvertently created an audit finding. As quality professionals, we know to document the deviation rationale, but sometimes those records aren't kept with the actual inspection records (only in an e-mail).

When is this not a good idea?

- For new production items (no actual inspection history)
- For new suppliers to your company
- For critical or high-risk components

Skip Lot, Reduced Inspection, and Tightened Inspection

There is a great deal already written on the topics of skip lot, reduced inspection, and tightened inspection so we'll keep this short. There are great opportunities to change the inspection level based on performance, but unless you have the right resources and automation behind this activity, it could become a huge resource impact.

The idea of not inspecting lots or changing the sample size takes some extra time that may be outside the "standard work" that will happen with the majority of the work. Anytime you deviate from the standard work there is a probability for an error to occur, and this is where the automation would be very helpful. The more mature quality systems have the ability to allow for parts to be identified for these various inspection levels, track the inspection history, and prompt the technician on what steps may occur.

If given the opportunity to pursue this versus supplier data and control plans, we would recommend the latter of the two since the bigger impact can be recognized. Supplier data allow confidence to be built with your supplier and its performance, and to identify candidates for process control plans at the supplier.

Determine Where You Would Like to Be in Your Value/Cost Proposition and By When

After the production levels have been stable (e.g., six to eight months), take a look at how effective the controls have been by examining some of the basic results that should be easily accessible:

- Inspection issues—have there been any issues at the supplier or at incoming?
- Production issues—have any major issues been identified during the production of the finished device? If so, do any of those issues point back to the controls that you put in place?

- Field issues—have any major issues been identified during the actual intended use of the finished device? Have there been any field recalls? If so, do any of those issues point back to the controls that you put in place?
- Based on the performance levels and the cost involved, are there any areas that change that have low risk of impacting the current model?

This information will allow you to see the different levels of controls and their effectiveness at detecting issues. Now it's time to see what controls can be moved closer to the biggest impact source. The work that has been done so far will allow your suppliers to take more responsibility for their product quality. This tool is called a process control plan.

Focusing on the Critical Few and Resources

When you start the work on the PCP activities, you need to make sure you have the resources to properly deploy this program. The rule of thumb for the ratio of supplier quality engineers to suppliers is 15:1, though that may be too high if your company makes only highly complex or critical devices such as CAT scanning equipment or implantable devices. Even if you are an "army of one," focus should be on the critical few suppliers. That still might mean 1 person may have 10 suppliers, so you have to spend your time appropriately.

In order to properly identify those suppliers, you have to look at your risk assessment documents (FMEA, fault tree analysis, and product risk assessment) and identify those components and suppliers that have the most risk. When we talk about risk, we are referring to the risk that could affect patient safety through a failure.

Process Control Plans

- How are they created?
- When should process control plans be created and where?
- What does the activity provide?

Process control plans are tools used to communicate process controls, frequency of inspection, and method of processes, change management levels, and contingency plans when failures occur. These are very common in the automotive industry, and more industries have incorporated these documents into their requirements. Based on the complexity and risk of the items, these control plans may take some time. So the question is, how do you get all the plans in place?

The controls required for each commodity can be grouped together, and the required controls can be as outlined in Table 5.8. Even if the risk is low or negligible, it's a good idea to have these commodities identified and controls defined. An external auditor reviewing your procedures will expect to see some level of detail of controls based on the levels. Also, it provides the rationale for why you may be focusing on category 1 and 2 suppliers more than the other levels.

Now that you have suppliers broken up in to smaller categories, it's easier to assign the amount of effort you put into creating the control plans for these items. By adding this level of categorization based on risk, you can better prioritize the implementation of control plans. If done correctly with the supplier, you can train them to help create them after you go through the initial items.

How Is the Control Plan Created?

The process steps for creating control plans are very similar to conducting an audit (see Table 5.9).

Table 5.8 Example of supplier category with controls using commodities.

Category	Commodities
Critical or high	Contract manufacturers Outsourcing of software used in manufacturing
Medium	Precision components Printed circuit board assemblies
Low	Noncritical components Off-the-shelf items, noncritical
Negligible	Janitorial services Office supplies

Category	Risk level	Commodities	Controls
1	High	Contract manufacturers Outsourcing of software used in manufacturing	Source inspection Process control plans Incoming inspection plans (LTPD 0.05%)
2	Medium to high	Precision components Printed circuit board assemblies	Process control plans Incoming inspection plans (LTPD 0.10%)
3	Low	Noncritical components	Incoming inspection plans (LTPD 0.15%)
4	Low	Off-the-shelf items, noncritical	Incoming inspection plans (LTPD 0.20%)

Table 5.9 Steps for creating the process control plan.

Process step	Conducting an audit	Creating a control plan
Prepare Gather documents	Review QA manual, work instructions, past audit issues Put together the initial checklist of items to cover	Review product specs, past performance, manufacturing documents, flowchart, yield reports, field reports Put together list of questions following the process
Conduct the assessment	Conduct the assessment at the site	Review the process and assess the actual controls and methods Identify key/critical process steps and assess the controls in place
Document results	Document the results	Document the results
Submit report	Submit the report	Submit the control pan
Assign corrective action	Assign corrective action	Assign corrective action
Follow up	Follow up	Follow up

Prepare

Get acclimated to the product:

- Read the product specification/product manual—what is the product supposed to do?
- Where is the product used? How is it used? By whom?
- Is it a stand-alone product, or does it work with something else?
- What safety concerns are called out?
- What is the performance so far? Incoming inspection, field returns, manufacturing yields? What failure types are identified in the FMEA/risk assessment documents?
- Review the manufacturing process flowchart—are the key inspection points identified? Are the procedures identified?
- Review the actual product—how is it packaged? How is it to operate?
- Is there an SME that could be a resource to review the product with you?

After completing this review, put together a list of questions that you want to review during the on-site assessment. It's recommended to take the flowchart and list each step out on a row. In the next column put down the information you want to review. Table 5.10 gives an example of the assessment document.

In this example, we will look at the loop used in implanting a mesh device for relieving incontinence. The method of manufacturing is as follows:

1. Cut braided wire to length
2. Crimp loop cannula
3. Crimp ball and shank
4. Cut tail tube
5. Inspect
6. Overmold
7. Assemble

Based on the associated design documents, design and process FMEAs, flowchart, and process documents, we would create the initial document prior to the on-site assessment (see Table 5.11).

Table 5.10 Example assessment document.

Process step	Document/ procedure number	Questions	Items to observe	Answers

Table 5.11 Draft assessment checklist.

Process step	Document/ procedure number	Questions	Items to observe	Answers
1. Cut braided wire to length	MFG 10123 DWG 11223 (wire)	How important is the wire length?		
2. Crimp loop cannula	MFG 10123 DWG 11012 (cannula)	How is the position of this crimp measured?		
3. Crimp ball and shank	MFG 10123 DWG 11223 (shank) DWG 11011 (ball)	Can the parts go together incorrectly?		
4. Cut tail tube	MFG 10123 DWG 11013 (assembly)	How critical is this dimension?		
5. Inspect	FM 1122 (record)	What is done with the data?		
6. Overmold	MFG 10124	Is the process outsourced or done internally? What controls are in place?		
7. Assemble	MFG 10125 DWG 11014 (assembly)	What is measured? What is critical at this point?		

Conduct the Assessment

The best way to assess the process is to go and see it for yourself. No matter how well the process is documented, you will see and hear more by observing the process firsthand. The best practice is to work with the supplier prior to the visit, share your assessment document with them, and ask them to schedule product to be observed. If production isn't scheduled at the time of your visit, ask if a sample build could be run.

Before you begin your assessment, spend time with the technicians and quality assurance (QA) people to show them the product. Explain how it's used and its intended use, and use any marketing documents to show them. Not many people know how the product is actually used, and they will appreciate the knowledge.

During your visit, spend time observing how components are handled, look for lot controls if needed, and watch how the technicians actually perform the activities. See if the work instructions are readily posted and if they reference them. Ask them questions directly regarding their activities, ask about problems they run into, and don't forget to thank them for their time (good manners go a long way).

During these activities, document what you observe on your assessment sheet. The questions you should be looking to answer are:

- *What is critical?* Are critical processes and QA inspections clearly identified for the person performing the work?

- *What process controls are in place?* If something goes wrong, will it be detected during the next operation? Is there any "mistake proofing" incorporated into the process, fixtures, or operations?
- *Where are these critical steps called out in the work instructions?*

A completed assessment document based on the observations is shown in Table 5.12.

The operations, documents, and tools highlighted are critical elements that could affect the product performance or part quality. The other steps are important but not everything is as important as these other steps. If these operations change, the supplier must provide the necessary justification to make the change and conduct the necessary validations to verify the product quality. From our experience, changes that seem benign to the technician cause the biggest product issues. It is not implied that people purposely make process changes to make bad product. Providing them with knowledge about how the product is actually used will help them think twice before making changes without going through the necessary due diligence.

Document Results, Assign Corrective Action

At the end of the assessment, discuss the results of the assessment with the supplier. Make sure to offer compliments where appropriate as well as identify areas for improvement and any necessary corrective action. Inadequate process controls are usually the result of "That's what we were told to do" after the design transfer to production. Data collection not being analyzed is generally the result of not knowing that the information could be used for advanced process controls. In the example, the results of the tensile testing had been collected for years, but no one had done any further analysis such as trending or process capabilities. In this case, the process capability was identified as adequate but could have been improved by making improvements to the wire used. The orientation of the wire into the fixture during step 2 directly affected the tensile results. Therefore, the supplier implemented process steps to show the proper orientation of the wire and trained all the technicians. This step became a critical process step.

Submit Report

After the corrective actions or process improvements are implemented, the initial control plan can be created and submitted to the supplier. The example document is shown in Table 5.13.

One means of control pointed out in the regulation is notification of change. We touch on this in Chapter 6 with regard to SQA, so we will not discuss in detail the FDA requirement. What we will discuss here is what happens when you don't have an SQA with the supplier or what happens if the supplier does not want to provide you with any advance notice. Then what do you do?

How do you ensure your supplier is not making changes to the product or services it is providing? Unless you are on-site all the time, it comes down to the relationship that you have with each of your suppliers. As part of the supplier evaluation/onboarding, you should provide to your supplier a change notification form listing the information needed for you to determine whether the change(s) may affect the quality of the finished device. Reference our example of a supplier change notification form on the CD accompanying this book. For consultants or contractors, you may include a phrase in the evaluation form they sign such as the following: *By signing this form you are agreeing to notify ABC of changes in the service so ABC can determine whether the changes affect the quality of a finished device.*

The types of changes that should be communicated to you from your supplier are those that could potentially affect the quality of the finished device; this also includes services. If you have a validated process at your supplier and the supplier decides to make changes to the process, the supplier should notify you in advance of the changes so you can determine whether the changes affect the quality of the finished device. In some cases you may only have to conduct verification, but in other instances you may have to complete a revalidation of the process.

Table 5.12 Completed assessment document.

Process step	Document/ procedure number	Questions	Items to observe	Answers
1. Cut braided wire to length	MFG 10123 DWG 11223 (wire)	How important is the wire length?	Are any inspection tools used?	The length is not critical since wire is cut off after overmolding.
2. Crimp loop cannula	MFG 10123 DWG 11012 (cannula) DHR 11112 TOOL 11112	How is the position of this crimp measured?	Are the parts clearly identified and traceable to a lot number? Is it recorded?	The lot numbers are recorded on the DHR. The crimp tool controls the position, which was validated during the initial process validation.
3. Crimp ball and shank	MFG 10123 – step 2.3, 5.6 DWG 11223 (shank) DWG 11011 (ball) TOOL 11112	Can the parts go together incorrectly?	Is their location controlled?	The process uses a fixture that was validated during the initial process validation.
4. Cut tail tube	MFG 10123 DWG 11013 (assembly)	How critical is this dimension?	Is this critical later in the process?	This dimension is not critical for processing.
5. Inspect	FM 1122 (Record) TOOL 11113	What is done with the data?	Are any samples tested?	Before each run, the crimping operation is tested on a tensile machine. The results are reviewed by QA before going to the next step.
6. Overmold	MFG 10124 SUPPLIER 1112 INCOMING 11112	Is the process outsourced or done internally? What controls are in place?	Where is the process step done?	Process step is outsourced to a local supplier. Supplier QA has a control plan in place and verifies the controls are being followed quarterly. Parts are verified during incoming inspection. No issues have been observed and no field failures have occurred in the last two years.
7. Assemble	MFG 10125 – step 2.6, 6.5 DWG 11014 (assembly) TOOL 11114	What is measured? What is critical at this point?	How is this item assembled?	The parts are assembled with a heat gun using an assembly fixture. The process step requires training the technician to make sure the parts are not overheated to achieve the bonding process. Visual standards are posted at the assembly bench. Training records confirm the technicians are properly trained.

Table 5.13 Process control plan.

Document number	Revision	Title	Relevant section
DHR 11112	B	DHR, loop	All
TOOL 11112	C	Crimp tool	All
MFG 10123	B	Crimp ball and shank	Step 2.3
FM 1122 (Record)	F	Inspection results	All
TOOL 11113	**B**	Tensile testing	Step 5.6
SUPPLIER 1112	N/A	Overmolding supplier	Change of supplier, process changes, or location of manufacturing
INCOMING 11112	C	Incoming procedure	All
MFG 10125	D	Assembly procedure	Steps 2.6, 6.5
TOOL 11114	B	Assembly tools	All

Another change you need to be aware of is a change to the material, especially if you are purchasing an off-the-shelf (OTS) product to use with your finished device. Services include things like sterilization, passivation, and anodizing, to name a few. To ensure that material has not been changed, you may want to request a certificate of analysis (CoA), not to be confused with a certificate of conformance (CoC). A CoA lists the physical properties of the product and is generally done by an outside lab. A CoC, on the other hand, is just a piece of paper from the supplier saying the product conforms to your specifications.

When you own the design, managing the change is much less complicated (or should be) than when you are purchasing an OTS product. Most of the time you are flowing the change down to your supplier(s) as opposed to your supplier flowing the change up. We will not go into the details of the change management process. We want to touch on key points like ensuring the new specifications are provided to the supplier and the supplier has adequate controls in place to flow these new specifications down to manufacturing. Be sure to cover work in process or any inventory the supplier may have. You may want to have a checklist of the documents you'll need to provide to your supplier after they have been updated; see Table 5.14 for an example.

For example, the change may not take effect until a certain date or certain lot/batch. All parties involved need to know when that date or lot/batch is so they can inspect the product to the correct specification revision. In some cases you may want the supplier to send back a change notification destroy order when all the previous specifications have been destroyed throughout the supplier's plant. One thing you don't want is to find obsolete versions of specifications being used.

What types of controls are needed when things don't go as planned? You may have a supplier that does not want to provide you with a change notification. It may be making an OTS product that is likely not intended for a medical device, but you have determined a need for it—for example, a standard spring used as a component in your finished medical device. In this case you will need to have many more internal controls in place as opposed to a mix of controls. Perhaps tightened inspection along with a CoA. Perhaps your own testing of the product (e.g., destructive) to ensure it meets your specifications or your intended use. This could be part of your incoming inspection or part of your in-process controls.

So what happens when products do not meet your specifications at your facility or your supplier's facility? As a medical device manufacturer you are required to have a procedure

Table 5.14 Supplier document checklist.

Updated documents provided to supplier	Yes or N/A
Specification/drawing	☐ Yes ☐ N/A
Parts lists (subcomponent)	☐ Yes ☐ N/A
Labeling and packaging specification	☐ Yes ☐ N/A
Instructions for use	☐ Yes ☐ N/A
Incoming inspection plans	☐ Yes ☐ N/A
In-process inspection plans	☐ Yes ☐ N/A
Final inspection plans	☐ Yes ☐ N/A
Other (describe)	☐ Yes ☐ N/A

for nonconforming product, so we will infer that is followed at your facility. However, if your supplier is not regulated by the ISO or FDA, it may not have a procedure covering nonconforming product. If the company is not making a custom component and you are purchasing an OTS product, more than likely you will never know. So, you will need to resort to recommendations stated under the change notification with regard to more internal controls.

When the supplier is manufacturing a product to your specification and it encounters nonconforming product that might require a deviation and/or concession, the supplier should not make that determination, particularly if rework or repairs are involved. The supplier does not have the responsibility or the expertise to determine whether the rework or repair adversely affects the product. That is the responsibility of the finished device manufacturer. If the supplier has experience in the medical device industry, it will likely be familiar with this and will probably have a sign-off for the customer. For those suppliers that are new to the industry, you may want to either provide them with your nonconforming product form or see if they can update theirs to include a sign-off by you.

A word of caution comes with regard to releasing product under concession (use "as is"). The FDA generally puts more scrutiny on product that is released that does not meet specifications but that you say is OK. When product is released under concession, it could raise questions as to who is not doing their job. The design engineer made the specifications for some reason, and then the product/material review board says that it's OK to release it. If the product is truly OK, then perhaps a reassessment of the specifications is needed, or perhaps product should not be released until it satisfies the requirements of the specifications.

An important thing to consider is if the supplier changes its senior management, you should understand the background of the senior management, as the decisions they make may affect the quality of your finished device.

In 2013 John was part of a consulting team that was cleaning up a recidivist warning letter. The company's CEO had no experience in the medical device industry, and he was hired to make the company look good on paper so it could be sold. His main goal was to reduce costs 20% across the board, including resources. Some of the first people to go were in quality. He was not the cause of all the previous warning letters, but he was part of management with executive responsibility and the ability to change the quality system, which can affect the quality of the finished device.

The following is taken from the FDA's *Compliance Program Guidance Manual,* Program 7382.845:

> The Recidivist Policy—Enforcement Strategy For Establishments With Repeated Violative Inspections
>
> Some establishments have a high rate of recidivism. They have developed a pattern of correcting violative conditions in response to a Warning Letter or other

> administrative/regulatory action, and usually maintain those corrections long enough to pass the follow-up inspection. When FDA next inspects the establishment (sometimes, as a follow-up to a recall), the investigator identifies similar conditions that again meet the criteria for Situation I. This tendency toward recidivism is often due to the failure of the establishment to have an effectively established quality management system being implemented. (US Food and Drug Administration 2011, p. 6)

Supplier Corrective Action Request (SCAR): When Should This Be Sent and Escalated?

A SCAR can be issued for audit findings and other supplier performance issues, but it should not be a surprise to the supplier when this occurs. Communication and explaining the reason and expectation will go a long way toward building a relationship with your supplier. Just by the name—SCAR—the perception is not good. However, the industry standard is to use this acronym, and since it's something that everyone understands, we'll keep it.

The million dollar question is, when do we issue a SCAR when the item is rejected during production, either at incoming inspection, in production, or from a customer complaint? The answer is, it depends.

There are many questions that have to be answered before you issue your supplier a SCAR:

- How critical is the item?
- What type of supplier is involved?
- Is this the result of a recall or product correction?
- What is the impact to the end customer?
- Is this a repeat occurrence? When was the last time this happened?
- What is the total cost of this rejection?
- Is this a long lead item?

These questions should help address 90% of the scenarios you encounter, but there may be other circumstances that need to be addressed for your specific company. These answers may not be useful in making the decision to issue a SCAR but are important information to know.

Risk-Based SCAR Decision

There are several ways to make the decision of when to issue a SCAR, and we would like to offer a solution using severity and occurrence. These are levels that have been created that need to be reviewed and adjusted to your company's situation and risk levels. Table 5.15 is the risk -based SCAR decision matrix that can be used as the foundation for making the decision while exceptions may be documented to explain other outcomes.

First identify the risk severity from the top of the matrix, which is based on the criteria outlined. Again, this information may be modified to best fit your company. Then, select the frequency of this issue specific with this supplier. Using the risk matrix portion, find the intersection of the severity and frequency to determine the action.

As an example, you may have a rejection that has a low risk and a first time frequency. In this case you would want to notify the supplier so they are aware of the issue. As another example, you may have a severity of critical and first time frequency, which would direct you to issue a SCAR. The rationale for this example is to make sure the supplier is taking corrective action because the severity of this failure could result in serious injury or death to a patient.

Table 5.15 Risk-based SCAR decision tool.

Description	Definition
Critical	• Performance impact, up to and including product failure with the potential for serious injury to the operator or patient* due to failure of product to meet performance specifications • Potential for death of the operator and/or patient* as a result of product failure • Impact to customer to fulfill production requirements • Critical risk to compliance with regulatory requirements including but not limited to product recall • Product returned from the customer due to a rejection at their location • Product from a critical or category 1 supplier • Reoccurrence after issue was identified previously and corrective action was not effective
Moderate	• Performance impact, up to and including product failure with the potential for injury to the operator and/or patient* that would not require medical intervention • Moderate risk to product or process and/or compromised product • Moderate risk to compliance with regulatory requirements including but not limited to internal audit nonconformance and supplier quality audit nonconformance • Significant scrap determined by supply chain • Significant process down time, long lead time items • Product from a category 2 supplier
Low	• Has little to no impact on production • Low scrap cost determined by supply chain • Product from a category 3 supplier
Negligible	• Minimal risk of injury to the operator and/or patient • Minimal risk to the product or process • No impact on product or process performance or safety • No impact on regulatory compliance

Frequency	
Description	**Quantitative likelihood**
Continually	Nonconformance with other products being provided by the same supplier
Frequently	Has occurred several times in the past 12 months
Occasionally	Nonconformance has not occurred in the past 12 months
Rarely	First-time occurrence of this nonconformance

Risk matrix				
	Negligible	**Low**	**Moderate**	**Critical**
Continually	SCAR	SCAR	SCAR and escalation	SCAR and escalation
Frequently	SCAR	SCAR	SCAR	SCAR and escalation
Occasionally	Notification	Notification	SCAR	SCAR
Rarely	Notification	Notification	SCAR	SCAR

*Patient impact is only applicable where the information is provided by the customer or where sites that manufacture finished products have the regulatory and clinical expertise.

Actions and Escalations

The risk matrix outlines the recommended actions that should be taken.

Please note that communication can be done via e-mail, phone calls, Skype, text, and so forth. However, you will find that the phone call will get the supplier's attention very quickly and you can always send an e-mail with the details.

Notification

- Nonconforming material e-mailed to supplier and call made to discuss containment plan at supplier
- Confirmation of issue by supplier should occur within 48 hours of issue being dispositioned as its responsibility

SCAR

- Nonconforming material e-mailed to supplier and call made to discuss containment plan at supplier
- Confirmation of issue by supplier should occur within 48 hours of issue being dispositioned as its responsibility
- SCAR e-mailed to supplier to document its investigation and action plan; formal response should be received within 10 business days

SCAR and Escalation

- Same actions listed in the SCAR action sections should be followed
- The quality and purchasing team should meet to determine whether any of the following actions need to be taken:
  - Require source inspection at supplier prior to shipment
  - Have supplier sort material on-site
  - Increase sampling plan levels at incoming inspection
  - Review quality performance of all other items from this supplier
  - Review quality performance of this supplier at other sites
  - Change supplier status on ASL (e.g., conditional) and reconsider supplier for future business
  - Perform for-cause audit at supplier

  Other team members should be included as needed, for example, production management, finance, and regulatory.

The results of these investigations should be reviewed, verified, and shared within the organization. This information is a feeder to the audit process, inspection process, and the scorecard/performance reporting.

Scorecards/Business Reviews

- Identify the metrics that are important and can be easily created (% acceptance, % on-time delivery, % SCAR response time)
- Data integrity importance (only reporting on supplier-related failures)
- Which suppliers should be part of this review

- What information should be shared or presented and the expected actions
- Frequency—quarterly versus annual

Scorecards and business reviews, when done correctly, can provide valuable information for your management reviews as well as your suppliers knowing just where they stand. But when they are done incorrectly, they are a total waste of vital resources. Furthermore, if the scorecard/business review paints a nice, rosy picture for the supplier and you are looking to discontinue use of the supplier due to its subpar performance, this may be a legal nightmare if in the supplier agreement/contract you state use of the supplier is based on the performance of the supplier as presented in the supplier's scorecard/business review.

John can recall an issue where the scorecards provided to the supplier indicated the supplier was in good standing in all the areas rated, but an individual within the purchasing department wanted to discontinue use of the supplier because he felt the supplier's quality was subpar. During the meeting with the manager of supplier quality and the purchasing manager of the major IVD manufacturer, the VP of sales from the supplier presented several years of scorecards indicating the supplier's performance not only was in good standing but also showed improvement over the past few years. The supplier's VP of sales was very much advocating for her company that if its performance was subpar, why was this not presented in the scorecards so they could have taken action to improve it? Needless to say, she was not 100% effective at presenting her case, as some business was lost by the supplier, but her point was well received that the data presented to the supplier need to be accurate. In this case the data were accurate, but the company lost out to politics and in the end wasted vital resources in a tool that was not used correctly or as intended.

Table 5.16 shows some advantages and disadvantages of using supplier scorecards. If you plan on using scorecards, it is very critical that you identify metrics that are important and can be easily created from data and not from opinions. One of the biggest issues often encountered with scorecards is adding subjectivity to the scorecard as opposed to quantitative data, such as the number of lots right as opposed to "they were not very nice to me." Data that go into the scorecards should be easily obtained and should not take days or weeks to gather and "scrub." It shouldn't take two weeks to gather the data and generate reports.

One of the biggest questions that faces every company is how often to provide the scorecard to the supplier. Frequency of the scorecard will depend on several factors, such as:

- How much data you want in your scorecard
- How many suppliers you want to provide with a scorecard
- How many resources are available (small vs. large company)
- How many resources are available at your supplier(s) (small vs. large company)

For larger companies that have the available resources, providing a scorecard on a quarterly basis is sufficient. For a small company that lacks resources, perhaps consider semiannually or annually. Regardless of the size of the company and resources, the information has to be concise and accurate, and provide performance information.

Table 5.16 Advantages and disadvantages of using supplier scorecards.

Advantages	Disadvantages
• Quick overview of supplier's performance • Compare against other similar suppliers • Way to track poor performing suppliers	• Data are not real time • Data are only as good as time spent tracking • Can be a resource drain

With regard to which suppliers get the scorecard/business review, this could be linked to which suppliers have supplier quality agreements or have been identified as "key suppliers"—critical and high-risk category suppliers.

Following are some commonly used metrics presented in scorecards/business reviews:

- Percent acceptance
- Percent on-time delivery
- Number of supplier corrective actions and/or number of nonconforming products

If you are looking to help the supplier improve its process and the supplier is willing to report it, scrap rate can be a very valuable metric, as this can drive the overall cost of the final product.

If you plan on using the scorecard where you plan to use both business metrics and quality metrics, it's best to use a weighting method for the categories. Figure 5.8 shows an example of a process that could be easily adapted.

As illustrated in the figure, there are three main categories by which suppliers are measured:

- Quality—50%
- Delivery—30%
- Cost and supply management initiatives (CSMI)—20%

Quality Category: Rating Criteria

The quality category comprises two components:

- Ratio of acceptance (ROA)—40%
- Quantity of SCARs issued—10%

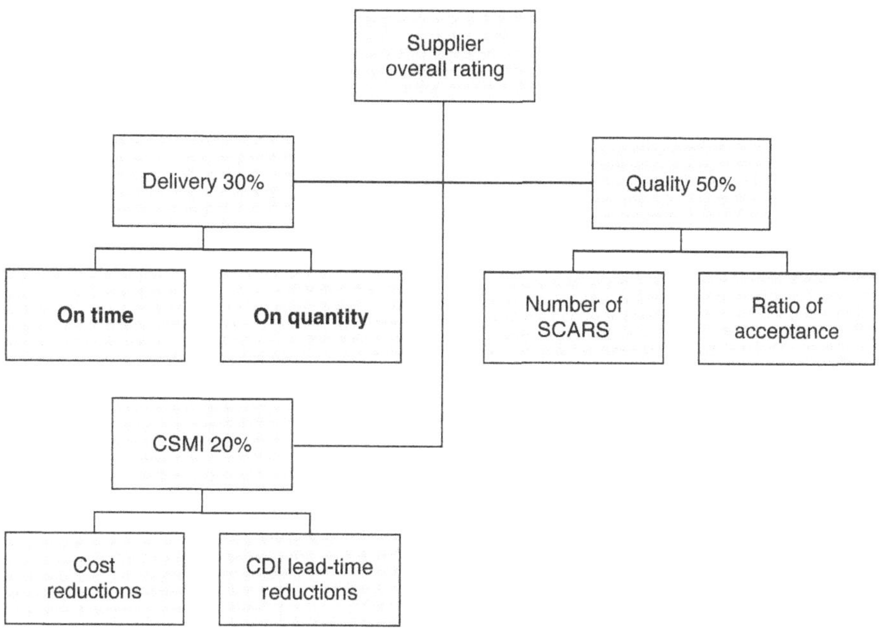

Figure 5.8 Supplier scorecard overview.

ROA is based on the number of lots accepted during the measurement period. This includes lots used in process manufacturing. (Note: measurement needs to distinguish between incoming and in-process acceptance/reject.)

The number of SCARs is determined by the number of SCARs assigned by Company XYZ's quality department during the period measured. This can be total SCARs or normalized based on the number of shipments. In the example shown in Table 5.17, the supplier's overall ROA is 97% and it has one SCAR. It would receive 46.3 points for quality ((97 × .4 = 38.8) + 7.5 for 1 SCAR).

Delivery Category: Rating Criteria

On-time delivery percentage has a window of five days early and zero days late to the due date. The on-time delivery percentage is determined by line items received on time divided by the number of line items due by the supplier for the month.

The on-quantity delivery is the percentage of all deliveries for the period received within the defined quantity limits. During this period the supplier was running at 95% for both on-time delivery and on-quantity delivery so it received a total of 28.50 points (95 × .15 = 14.25 + 95 × .15 = 14.25), as displayed in Table 5.18.

CSMI Category: Rating Criteria

CSMI is measured by mutually agreed-upon cost savings and supply chain targets. The cost savings is year-over-year price reductions. Supply chain measures are lead-time reduction and inventory reduction. Company XYZ uses the phrase "consumable days of inventory" (CDI) for inventory turns. In the example shown in Table 5.19 the supplier stated it would reduce cost by 5% and lead time by 5%. It made both targets so it received the full allotted points of 20 for this area (100 × .20 = 20).

Table 5.17 Supplier's quality score.

ROA count	Points (40%)	# of SCARs per X shipments	Points (10%)
98%–100%		0–10	
91%–97%	38.8	1–7.5	7.5
86%–90%		2–5	
Below 85%		3–2.5	

Table 5.18 Supplier's delivery score.

On-time delivery	Points (15%)	On-quantity delivery	Points (15%)
95%–100%	14.25	95%–100%	14.25
90%–94%		90%–94%	
85%–89%		85%–89%	
80%–84%		80%–84%	
Below 80%		Below 80%	

Table 5.19 Supplier's CSMI score.

CSMI measurement	Points (20%)
90% or higher of agreed-upon targets	20
80%–89% of agreed-upon targets	
70%–79% of agreed-upon targets	
60%–69% of agreed-upon targets	
Below 60% of agreed-upon targets	

Table 5.20 Supplier's overall rating.

Supplier's overall rating	Total points
Preferred: 92–100	94.8
Acceptable: 83–91	
Probationer: 75–82	

The supplier's overall rating is a summation of all the categories. Based on the supplier's rating, it would be classified as a preferred supplier, as its points tally up to 94.8 (46.3 + 28.5 + 20), as shown in Table 5.20.

Communication/Escalation Plans

Communication plays a key role in any relationship, especially in your interaction with suppliers. The following is a high-level overview of things to consider when communicating with your suppliers.

- Brief overview of communication
- Keeping your communication and contact list current (people leaving and may not be notified)
- What information should be shared, what is the frequency, and can you sustain it?
- Escalation of issues—who should be called and what is the expectation on responding?
- SCARs—when should notification versus action be decided? What risk factors should be used?

Communication, communication, communication. One of the key aspects of any relationship is centered on communication and managing the communication regardless of its type. For instance:

- *The Good:* Hey Supplier XYZ, you guys are doing great. Keep up the good work.
- *The Bad:* Hey Supplier XYZ, I have an issue with the last shipment I want to discuss.
- *The Ugly:* Hey Supplier XYZ, since being on probation you have not shown any improvement, so we will have to terminate our relationship.

By no means will this be an in-depth course on communication, but understanding that communication has two parts—transmitters and receivers—can help in the accuracy of information transmitted to and received from both parties.

Transmitters can be in the fashion of oral (talk to the individual) or written (drawings, specifications, SCAR, e-mail, etc.). We are conveying the information to the other party so they can receive it.

Receivers follow a similar fashion of oral (hearing/listening to the individual talk) or written (reading/interpreting the drawings, specifications, SCAR, e-mail, etc.).

When communicating, the following should be considered:

- Importance of terminology between supplier and manufacturer to reduce errors, for example, make sure a widget is a widget
- Manufacturers should communicate to suppliers clear and concise requirements and allow feedback from the suppliers without any repercussions
  - Dimensions over use of words such as "long enough," "small enough," "easy to use," etc.
- Suppliers should understand the information being provided by the manufacturer and be allowed to seek clarity when requirements are ambiguous
- Standardize terms
  - 21 CFR 820.3—Definitions
  - ISO 9000:2005, Quality management systems—Fundamentals and vocabulary

Another important aspect, especially with larger suppliers, is to keep the contact list up to date. This applies to suppliers as well when you are supporting larger medical device manufacturers. If you have a good rapport with your supplier/manufacturer, this may not be as big of a concern, but it's always best to ensure that you have the latest information on your contacts and any backup.

Scorecards were discussed earlier as a means of communication with your supplier about its overall performance. Another means of communication is through the nonconformance process, where you are dealing with a specific issue. Before you issue a supplier a nonconformance, consider the following:

- Importance of alignment of supplier and customer CAPA processes and activities
- Does not mean force your process on the supplier
- Ensure understanding of terminology and priority in dealing with CAPA (reference cited material above)
- Allow openness for supplier to make recommendations for preventive actions

When it's time to use the nonconformance process to address an issue that has occurred, you should be concise yet detailed enough in relaying the information so that the supplier can take action:

- Be very specific about the nonconformance
  - Part number/DWG no.
  - Quantity
  - Lot no.
  - PO
- Cite the specification not being met, for example,
  - The OD of the part XYZ-1 does not meet the drawing spec of 1.500 +/– .005
  - Of the 30 parts measured, 10 parts fell outside the spec (list the measurements of the 10 parts)

One of the most important things to do when sending product back to the supplier for it to investigate the issue is to segregate the parts. Do not just put them back in with the conforming product so the supplier has to reinspect all the parts to find the nonconforming product.

Note that not everything needs to be handled via the SCAR process. If nonconforming product is involved, then, yes, the SCAR process should be used as a means to meet regulatory obligations to notify and evaluate the need for an investigation. If the supplier has some minor documentation errors that do not affect the product or the traceability of the product, one way to handle the situation is to make a phone call and track the number of occurrences. If you see a negative trend when tracking the issues, then you should consider using the SCAR process to address the issue.

From time to time you will run across a supplier that just refuses to play nice. It's important to have an escalation process in place when dealing with this type of supplier. Perhaps you should see what type of escalation process you currently have in place. Some key factors to consider are:

- Understanding when and how to escalate
- Used as a last resort to resolve conflict between supplier and manufacturer
- Should have a trigger indicating when to escalate to management

If the relationship with your supplier does not improve, then consider your termination process with the supplier. Refer to Chapter 7 for supplier termination recommendations.

SUMMARY/TAKEAWAY

- Following the steps outlined in this chapter, you can design and implement effective controls that make logistical sense and are robust. The process control plan becomes the record of the work and can be updated as needed.
- Implementing controls at your facility through receiving inspection activities can be done in different ways, from incoming inspection to process control plans and process audits.
- The measurement of the controls can be determined through the cost of quality model.
- Creating the strategic supplier map will help with making a decision on risk mitigation and the intent of pushing the right controls to the closest point possible—at the supplier.
- Communication with your suppliers is critical throughout the relationship.

6

Controls: What Are Contractual Requirements?

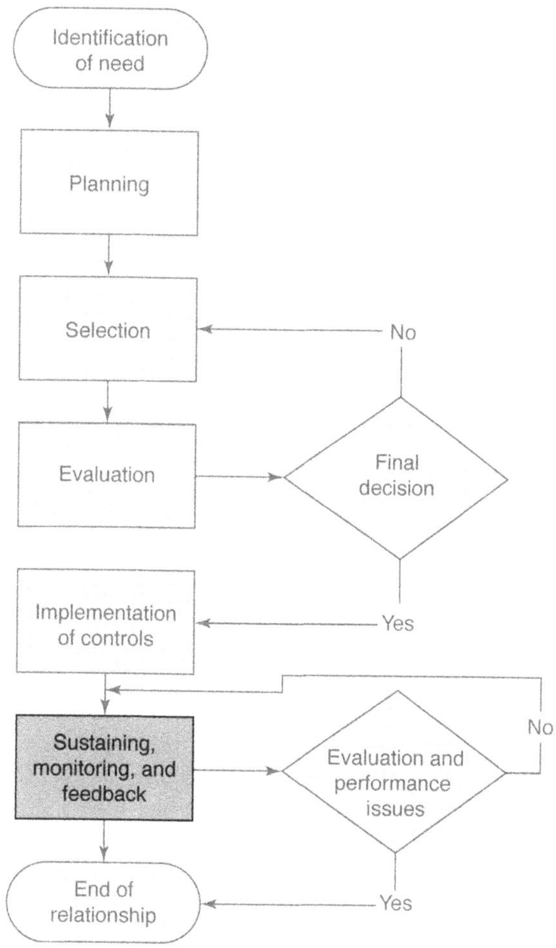

CONTRACTS/AGREEMENTS

Maintaining quality agreements with multiple suppliers can be challenging, to say the least, since there will be inevitable inconsistencies from one document to the next. At worst, a poorly understood and executed agreement can be a legal, regulatory, or customer relations liability. You may be working with a company in a different country with different regulators.

If you don't have a process in place for quality agreements, the first thing to do is to perform a gap assessment against the basic requirements (suggested elements to include, besides the notification of change requirement, appear later in the chapter). The inconsistencies need to be addressed by the original equipment manufacturer, as well as a review of what is being reported by the FDA during the warning letter citations. This review of what is being issued now will allow you to act proactively and potentially avoid those issues showing up in a letter to your company.

An agreement should outline the key roles and responsibilities of the parties. Metrics and due dates should be clearly identified to avoid scope creep. From the contract manufacturer's point of view, if your customer makes requests that were not agreed upon in the initial document, the agreement should be renegotiated. Remember, the supplier quality agreement (SQA) is a two-way document that should identify key suppliers and indicate whom to notify if the FDA shows up for an inspection. You don't want to be in a situation where someone from your company is unable to answer the agency's questions or, worse, answers them incorrectly. This section of the book takes a proactive look at SQAs.

THE MAIN TOPICS COVERED IN THIS CHAPTER

- Review of the FDA requirements for agreements
- What the FDA is citing in warning letters for agreements
- Elements of an SQA

Supplier quality is becoming more complex with the increase in outsourcing and virtual manufacturers. All throughout the supply chain (receiving raw material to distribution), it's becoming more difficult to track back to the actual manufacturer. There has been a drive by the FDA for the past several years to increase focus on supplier controls. As we saw from the data presented in Chapter 1, not much has changed going back to 2004.

Before we go into detail about supplier agreements, we would like to provide a brief overview of the FDA requirements with regard to quality agreements—or to be more precise, "notification of change." Under 21 CFR 820.50(b) the FDA does not call it a "quality agreement" but states that "where possible," purchasing documents should include "an agreement that the suppliers, contractors, and consultants agree to notify the manufacturer of changes." As with most things, industry has coined it "quality agreement"; thus, it's an industry norm. To be more harmonized with the FDA's subclause, ISO 13485:2016 has adopted similar verbiage with regard to notification of change.

If you conducted a search in the QSReg for the use of "where possible," you would find it comes up only once under this subpart, as opposed to the phrase "where appropriate," which is used 15 times throughout the QSReg. Referring back to the scope under 21 CFR 820.1(a)(3), the FDA clearly states that when it determines that a requirement is qualified by "where appropriate," it deems it to be appropriate unless the manufacturer can document justification otherwise.

So why is it different here? If we review the preamble we can see that industry provided the FDA feedback with regard to making it a requirement that "all" suppliers provide a notification of change. Industry feedback in comment #111 stated this puts "undue burden on suppliers and inhibits their ability to make minor adjustments within the parameters of agreed upon specifications and quality requirements."

As pointed out in the preamble (comment #111), and which we agree with, this is true when it's a custom device or custom component where the medical device manufacturer holds the design. However, when it's OTS, the medical device manufacturer has much less control over the OTS manufacturer with regard to making changes and notifying you of those changes. Therefore, the medical device manufacturer must impose other types of controls to ensure that if changes occur it can determine whether the changes affect the quality of the finished device. Although not a foolproof one, a control could be to confirm the part number and revision level at incoming inspection. Another control might include more detailed inspection or testing at incoming or during assembly/manufacturing. We have experienced this from both aspects where some OTS manufacturers will provide you written notification of change while others will not. It's been our experience that the larger the OTS manufacturer, the less likely you are to get a notification of change agreement, thus causing you to have more stringent internal controls.

Now that we have reviewed the requirements of the regulation with regard to notification of change, let's take a look at what the FDA is actually citing medical device manufacturers for in warning letters with regard to their SQAs. The following are excerpts from FDA warning letters issued to device manufacturers for lack of adequate quality agreements with their suppliers:

> Specifically, a supplier agreement has not been established between your firm and:
> a) The [redacted] to define quality system responsibilities such as finished device packaging and shipping. Requirements such as temperature and humidity control during transit and storage have not been defined.
> b) [redacted] to define quality system responsibilities such as complaint handling and MDR reporting.

> Your response is not adequate because you do not address the lack of a documented agreement between your firm and your contract laboratory that includes the requirements to be met by that supplier.

> Your firm's management stated that there were no sections in the contract that define how complaint handling is to be handled.

> The agreement with [redacted] does not address complaint handling, medical device reporting, labels/labeling content, product recall, or maintenance of device history records.

> The agreement with [redacted] does not address product design changes, complaint handling, medical device reporting, product recall, or maintenance of device history records.

> The agreement with [redacted] does not address product design changes, complaint handling, medical device reporting, recalls, label/labeling content, or maintenance of device history records. Additionally, the agreement is not signed and dated.

As you can see from the examples, and depending on the risk associated with the product or service, the FDA is looking for more detailed quality agreements.

So where do we go from here? What is adequate and what is not adequate? Is it necessary to cover quality system elements when the supplier's quality management system is compliant with ISO or FDA QSReg?

Contracts and quality agreements act as two-way communication between the supplier and manufacturers on how they conduct business in order to prevent or reduce issues between the two companies.

Contracts are the legally binding agreement, generally focusing on the business aspects. Quality agreements are more detailed with regard to requirements of the product/service or details about manufacturing and quality requirements of the medical device. A contract may just state that the supplier must be compliant with a certain quality system, without going into the details of who, what, when, how, and why.

A good contract will have a quality agreement either attached as an appendix or developed as a separate document. We have experience with both and prefer having the quality agreement as a separate document, as this makes it much easier to manage between the actual contributors to the process.

It's critical that up-front expectations of the supplier and the manufacturer be well documented and maintained throughout the life cycle of the product/service to ensure customers' expectations are met; in some cases, regulatory obligations are also addressed as cited in the warning letters.

Keep in mind that if your supplier is registered with the FDA, the SQA does not replace the supplier's regulatory obligations to be compliant with the FDA's QSReg. It should be a supplement to the supplier's quality management system to help define the responsibilities between the finished device manufacturer and the supplier (contract manufacturer).

Deciding whether an SQA is product specific or supplier specific might be based on the amount of product you are getting from the supplier. If you are buying a few items (custom components or finished devices), you may want to write a supplier agreement for each product. On the other hand, if you are procuring a large variety of products, for example, labeling/packaging, then you may want to write the agreement to be supplier specific. We have experience with both types of quality agreements and for the given situation they both work just fine.

Due to the time and resource commitments involved in developing and maintaining an SQA, it's recommended to focus on the vitally few suppliers. For most other suppliers, having a change notification form should suffice. This also includes consultants.

WHY DO I NEED THIS?

If the QSReg states that you only need to have a "change notice" with suppliers, why do you need to develop a more complex document? We feel the top reasons you should develop and maintain an SQA, besides the regulatory requirements, are as follows:

- Alignment of supplier and manufacturer goals and objectives pertaining to conformity requirements
- Clear delineation of quality responsibilities between parties
  - Critical to maximize efficiency
  - Provide quality products
  - Minimize miscommunication and inaccurate assumptions
- Include elements not called out or lacking detail in a contract (supply agreement)

WHAT IS IT?

As stated previously, the SQA details quality requirements that establish and maintain the systematic business relationship between a key/critical supplier and the medical device manufacturer. Depending on the complexity of the product or service, the SQA may affect the cost and scheduling.

WHAT MUST IT DO?

The SQA should be in agreement with other contracts, such as:

- Purchase order
- Supply agreement
- Manufacturing agreement
- Business contract

WHAT CONTENT IS NEEDED?

If we think about the basic information gathering framework we all learned as kids—who, what, when, where, how, and why—we can apply that to the contents of the SQA. When developing your SQA with your suppliers, ask the following questions: Who will do what? What will be done? When will it be done? Where will it be done? How will it be done? Why will it be done? We will discuss each of these shortly.

The contents of the SQA, at a minimum, should cover the following:

- Roles and responsibilities—use of organizational chart is best
- Key contacts and contract information
- Scope of products or services covered
- Controls
- Compliance and all expectations
- Accountability and escalations
- Approvals
- Periodic review

We ran across the following broad statement in an SQA we were reviewing for a client. This statement was under a subclause related to cGMP practices:

> COMPANY is responsible for ensuring that it conducts any Quality System Regulation related activities in reasonable compliance with FDA's requirements as necessary.

Because this statement is so broad, it is open to interpretation on both sides as to what it really means. We feel one of the key elements of the SQA is that both companies understand who is responsible for what and that it's clearly defined and not left open to interpretation. The SQA should avoid assumptions, miscommunication, misunderstanding, inappropriate expectations, and so on. Other things to watch out for are not addressing critical business and quality needs, not leveraging what the contract manufacturer has in place, treating all suppliers the same (one size does not fit all), and not educating suppliers on your product or how it's used and why it's important to manufacture product to your specifications.

One of the best methods of achieving a clearly defined SQA is to keep the content basic and simple to understand. Using tools like the five Ws and one H can help us construct the SQA. Remember to have a template as a starting point and add to or take away based on the risk associated with the product.

WHO WILL DO IT?

- Company or supplier
  - If both, describe division of responsibilities
  - Most common would be a contract sterilizer
  - Specific department/person
- Approval authority
- Training/certification requirements

For Example: Design Controls

ABC is responsible for design controls and may request assistance from the supplier as needed. The official device history file (DHF) resides at ABC and all design changes are the responsibility of ABC.

WHAT NEEDS TO BE DONE?

- Describe activity
- Appropriate level of detail for clarity
- Reference applicable documents
  - Specifications
  - SOPs/work instructions (WIs)
  - Forms
  - Standards

For Example: Customer Expectations and Metrics

- 90% of lots will not require a deviation resulting from supplier-related issues for release to the market
- Supplier will develop a root cause analysis and corrective action plan for consumer-reported product nonconformities
- 100% of lots will be shipped on time

WHEN WILL IT BE DONE?

- Prior to shipment
- Periodically based on time
- Every lot
- Only when specified by the company
- Triggering event
- Prior to a specific operation or activity
- Time frames for responses/info exchange:
  - Nonconforming material report (NCMR)
  - Corrective action requests
  - Complaints

For Example: Metrics Reporting

The performance metrics shown in Table 6.1 will be compiled by the fifth working day of each month for the previous month.

Table 6.1 Example metric responsibility table.

Metric	Responsible for collecting data
Lots (released to market) right first time (lots released by ABC without deviation)	ABC QC
Product complaints	ABC QC
On-time shipments	ABC launch support
For each lot manufactured: a) Final manufactured lot size b) Percent yield through the in-line tester c) Number of pens released to market (less five house samples) d) Number of open deviations	Supplier GM or designee

WHERE WILL IT BE DONE?

- At the supplier's facility
- At the purchaser's facility
- At another location
- Controlled environment/clean room

For Example: Release for Distribution

ABC is responsible for the final release of finished medical devices for distribution. Final lot disposition will take place at ABC.

HOW WILL IT BE DONE?

- Procedures
- Forms
- Test methods
- Equipment
- Visual aids/examples
- Standards

For Example: Supplier Evaluation and Continuous Monitoring

Procedures will be in place that meet the requirements of 21 CFR Part 820.50. Supplier will monitor the performance of its suppliers supplying material for use in ABC products. ABC quality, at the request of the supplier, can assist when needed.

WHY WILL IT BE DONE? (NOT EVERY SQA ELEMENT REQUIRES A WHY)

- Regulations
- Procedures

- Other agreements
  - Manufacturing agreement
  - Supply contract
  - Purchase order

The primary reason why we do most of the things we do is to satisfy our regulatory obligations as medical device manufacturers. The "why" is not explicitly written into the SQA, but it should be communicated to the supplier during your initial contact and you should periodically remind the supplier why it is doing things a certain way. It is very important for a supplier new to the industry to understand that people's lives may be at risk if it deviates from the specifications or requirements.

SQA ELEMENTS

A good starting point for the SQA is to have a template with common verbiage that you add to or take away based on the risk associated with the product or service you are procuring. The goal is not to make it "one size fits all," but to have a recipe to pick and choose which elements will be included based on the risk associated with the product or service. The SQA should define who approves it and when it's to be periodically reviewed, and apply any needed updates.

Approvals should involve comparable individuals from the supplier and the manufacturer (e.g., quality manager, production manager, and engineering). We recommend conducting a periodic review at least annually to ensure adequacy of the agreement. This review should coincide with the supplier audit, and deviations from the SQA should be referenced in the audit report. If updates are needed, they should be identified and approved by the supplier and the manufacturer.

An example of a basic SQA template you can use to develop your own template is located on the CD accompanying this book. Again, the goal is not to make this "one size fits all," but a recipe that goes above the requirement of a change notification in 21 CFR 820.50(b).

The following are examples of key elements you should include in your SQA (as pointed out previously, the FDA has been citing companies for more than what is called out in the QSReg under 820.50(b):

1. Introduction and approvers
2. Quality requirements
3. Management responsibilities
4. Customer expectations
   - 4.1. Metrics
5. Design controls
6. Audits
   - 6.1. Internal
   - 6.2. External (customer and suppliers)
   - 6.3. Allowing access for unannounced audits (CE mark product only)
   - 6.4. Agency notifications
7. Documentation/records
   - 7.1. Who, what, when, where, and how maintained
   - 7.2. Device history file (DHF)

   7.3. Device master record (DMR)
   7.4. Device history record (DHR)
8. Supplier evaluation and continuous monitoring
9. Material control and traceability
   9.1. Incoming material inspections
   9.2. In-process controls
   9.3. Inspection and test methods (final acceptance)
   9.4. Release for distribution
10. Nonconforming product
   10.1. Rework/repair
11. Validation
12. Change control
13. Packaging/labeling
14. Supplier corrective action
15. Product complaints/product recalls/MDR
16. Installation and servicing, where applicable

Sterilization Verbiage

Refer to the example on the CD accompanying this book.

Compliance with Laws

Each of the parties agrees at all times to conduct its operations in compliance with the applicable requirements of 21 CFR Part 801.150—*Medical Devices: Processing, labeling or packaging*, 21 CFR Part 820—*Quality System Regulation*, or any successor regulations as well as any other applicable laws and regulations.

SUMMARY/TAKEAWAY

- Review of warning letters reveals the FDA is putting much more scrutiny on SQAs; depending on the risk associated with the product or service, the FDA is looking for much more detailed quality agreements.
- Start with an SQA template and write the agreement commensurate with the risk of the product. Not all suppliers will need a detailed SQA, but all suppliers should receive a change notice form to provide to you for changes to their product or service.
- The SQA should define critical up-front expectations of the supplier and the manufacturer, and these should be maintained throughout the life cycle of the product or service to ensure customers' expectations are met and in some cases regulatory obligations are addressed.

- For suppliers registered with the FDA, the SQA does not replace the supplier's regulatory obligations to be compliant with the FDA's QSReg. It should be a supplement to the supplier's QMS to help define the responsibilities between the finished device manufacturer and the supplier (contract manufacturer).
- When possible, have comparable individuals at each company review and approve the SQA.
- Remember to have an agreement in place that covers the elements of 801.150(e) when shipping product that is to be sterilized to and from your sterilizer.
- Finally, the SQA should be periodically reviewed and updated as needed.

7

Supplier Consolidation: Do We Still Need Them?

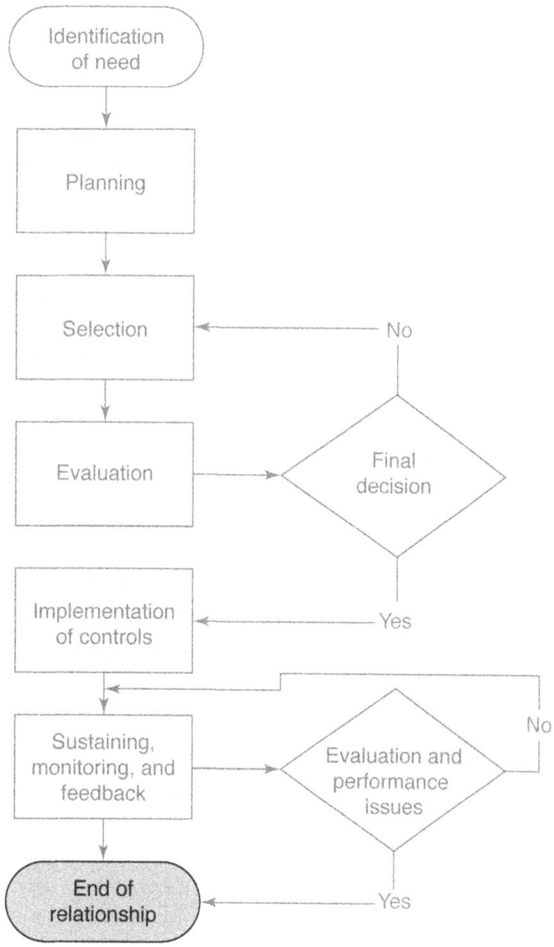

MAIN TAKEAWAYS FROM THIS CHAPTER

- Creating a process to determine consolidation of suppliers for business or performance reasons
- Reviewing the total cost of ownership (TCO) model for supplier consolidation purposes
- Once the decision is made regarding the consolidation, creating a well-thought-out implementation plan
- Creating a process to deactivate suppliers without disapproving them, and bring them back without delays if needed

TERMINATION VERSUS CONSOLIDATION

One of the best ways to think of ending a supplier relationship is likening it to an investment that is costing you money. You can continue to invest in this poorly performing asset and lose money, or you can put your investment into a better payoff.

The benefits of consolidation are simple:

- Stronger relationships can be built when you have fewer suppliers
- Improved relationships and fewer suppliers allow quality to focus on issues quicker and reduce the impact on production
- Larger discounts can be achieved with larger buying power
- Shipping and freight costs can be better managed

This chapter discusses the need to review and consolidate the supplier base for business and performance reasons. "Termination" or "end of relationship" may be too sharp, so for our purposes we will look at it as a consolidation effort. Is termination the same as consolidation? No, there is a difference based on the reasons for ending the business relationship. Either way, this chapter will provide some best practices on the implementation plan. It is important to consider this since your suppliers come with a cost and effort associated with onboarding and maintaining them.

Consider the owner of a rental car company who has enough cars to address the capacity needs but does not want too many cars sitting idle for an extended period while still paying for insurance, cleaning, and maintenance (e.g., oil changes, new tires). Say this rental car company is located in an area where there are harsh winters, like the New England area. It is not very practical for the rental car company to rent convertibles or rear-wheel-drive vehicles since most people are accustomed to front-wheel-drive or all-wheel-drive vehicles in snow. So, instead of selling these vehicles, the owner decides to store them in a garage and reduce the insurance coverage, thus reducing overall business expenses. Once better weather comes around, the owner can take these assets out of storage and have them back in the fleet and ready for customers in a short time.

Using this same scenario for your supplier base, you may want to review the number of similar suppliers and see if you have too many of one type. Do you need 45 machine shops? Do you represent less than 10% of one of these suppliers? There may be some suppliers that were selected for a project that is no longer in production, but you don't want to end the business relationship. How do you manage those suppliers without going through the entire approval process again?

START WITH THE END IN MIND: WHAT IS THE GOAL?

As quality professionals we know that if you can't measure it, you don't have a process. Without realistic goals or defined outcomes, you can spend a great deal of time without making any progress. So by starting with some agreed-upon goals and ground rules for this program, there will be less distraction that can derail your progress.

Here are some examples of ground rules:

- All the supplier data will be verified to be accurate and updated in the primary source of the information (e.g., enterprise resource planning [ERP], an access database, or some other web-based software system).
- Make sure all suppliers are assigned to the correct commodity group(s).
- We will have the proper representatives from each functional group (manufacturing, operations, supply chain, regulatory, purchasing, and quality). When we come to an issue that cannot be resolved by the team, the president will have the final decision. Once the decision is made, the team will honor it and proceed without any reservation.

- Some examples of goals are:
  - We will reduce our total number of suppliers by 10%, and our overall stretch goal is 15%.
  - We will reduce our overall supplier-related expenses by 20% by the end of Q1 2017.

SUPPLIER CONSOLIDATION: HOW DO I START THE ANALYSIS?

Recall the supplier scorecard discussed in Chapter 5. When done correctly, this is a great starting point. By combining your ASL with your supplier performance metrics into one spreadsheet, you can have all the data in one easy-to-read place.

Consider the following list of values as a baseline for this analysis (these values may be different based on your systems and the available information):

- Supplier name (full name as it comes out of your ERP system or your purchasing process)
- Supplier number (unique value)
- Location (city, state, country)
- Commodity (machining, packaging, printed circuit boards)
- Supplier category/level (critical, high, medium)
- Critical supplier (yes/no)
- Approval status (approved, conditional, inactivated)
- Initial evaluation method (on-site audit, survey)
- Initial evaluation date
- Last evaluation method (last evaluation done by an on-site audit, survey, etc.)
- Last evaluation date
- Supplier performance (from Chapter 5)—quality and delivery
- Total $ spent in the last 18 months
- For multiple sites, identify which sites use this supplier
- Part numbers associated with that specific supplier or supplier number
- Specific programs associated with this supplier
- Any regulatory-associated information (part of premarket approval [PMA], 510(k), etc.)
- Supplier's revenue in the last two years

There may be cases when you receive components from the one supplier that has multiple manufacturing sites. It's important to have a different supplier number for each site or someone to distinguish each location. At some point you may not want to continue working with all the supplier sites and having these details will be important.

The same applies if your company has multiple manufacturing sites and those sites share the same suppliers. Here's a situation where having that granularity is important. You don't want to shut off a supplier entirely if it is a critical supplier for one of your plants. This will be helpful when we discuss implementation strategies later in this chapter.

Data integrity is critical, and if you don't address it now, it will only make this analysis more challenging later. In larger companies, one of the greatest opportunities is to clean up duplicate data, as the supplier may have been entered several times with small deviations in its name. Jim can recall one company that had 17 different records for the same supplier! Each manufacturing site was allowed to enter its own data into the ERP system, and no one had checked to see if the supplier was already in the system. Simple variations of the name (abbreviations, spelling errors, and incomplete names) created huge data integrity issues.

SUPPLIER CONSOLIDATION: INITIAL BRAINSTORMING DISCUSSION

A spreadsheet of your suppliers will allow you to see the big picture as well as how many suppliers you have on your ASL. After you pull these data together, sit down with the project team and ask some basic questions:

- How many suppliers do we have for the same commodity? Is that too many? Is that enough to handle the capacity needed?
- Which suppliers have great or poor performance? Does this reflect the internal customers and their perceptions?
- Which suppliers are easy or difficult to work with from purchasing, quality, and operations perspectives?
- How much money are you spending with each supplier? Is there any correlation to its performance?
- How far away are your suppliers from your manufacturing or distribution locations? Who is paying for all the shipping and freight expenses?
- Are there any suppliers that would raise a significant regulatory impact if they were changed?
- Do we represent more than 40% of any of our supplier's business?
- Have any of these suppliers shown up in any media or business trade publications? Did an announcement of acquisition get published? Is that one of your competitors?

Sometimes these conversations can identify issues that you may not have known about, or there may not have been any data published for you to know. As a supplier quality professional, you'll hear from operations if it is not pleased with a supplier; but does everyone know that a specific supplier is part of FDA or MHLW (Minister of Health, Labour and Welfare) regulatory submission, and that in order to change that supplier, the cost associated with submitting those changes to regulators may be pricey.

SUPPLIER CONSOLIDATION: DATA ANALYSIS WITH TOTAL COST OF OWNERSHIP (TCO) MODELS

During these conversations with the other company functions, it's best to come up with a priority matrix to establish what criteria are more important than others. For example, which is more important to your company—total dollars spent with the supplier or total cost of shipping expenses? Poor performance or the cost of validation/regulatory filing expenses associated with changing the supplier?

In order to compare all these suppliers, review all suppliers individually but also in groups by supplier commodity. The reason is that in an aggregate view there may be some outliers that look really poor, but when compared with similar suppliers within the same commodity group they appear to be consistent.

There are many models and published studies from purchasing and supply chain professional groups, and the simple calculation that can be used for this analysis is (Table 7.1):

$$TCO = A_1 * A_2 * A_3 * A_4 \ldots$$

Where A_x is the key attribute and all the values are consistent with the weighting factors.

Table 7.1 How to use the TCO calculation.

Attribute	How to calculate it	How to assign a weighting factor
A_1—Cost of quality	Look at the supplier's overall reject rate as a percentage of all parts or lots received. Use the percent defective as a multiplier to identify the suppliers that are creating more expenses for rejections.	If the supplier has 100% quality, then the factor would be one. If it's 95%, then the factor would be 1.05.
A_2—Cost of delivery performance	Look at the supplier's overall on-time delivery rate as a percentage of all parts or lots received. Use the percent late as a multiplier to identify the suppliers that are creating more expenses for late deliveries.	Similar to quality, if the supplier has had 100% on-time delivery, then the factor would be one. If it has had poor delivery performance, such as 85%, then the factor would be 1.15.
A_3—Cost of inventory	If inventory turns are already calculated, then use those numbers. If not, then look at the percentage of shipments that can be delivered directly to the manufacturing area (JIT). Look at this like aging of products you have that you're not using but still have in your inventory (if shipments can't be determined, use cost of inventory).	Higher inventory turns are better, so this weighting is the inverse of the to previous calculations: 1–3 turns, factor = 2 4–6 turns, factor = 1.5 7–11 turns, factor = 1 >12 turns, factor = 0.5 The same weighting factor should be applied to % of shipments or cost of inventory. The less % than can be used directly to manufacturing or the higher the cost of inventory is part of the "hidden factory costs."
A_4—Cost of freight/shipping	Add freight and shipping costs and divide the total cost by the total number of units shipped. This will give you the transportation cost per unit.	Use a Pareto chart to look at the results. Scale of 1–3, 1 being no cost associated and 3 being the most cost. 1 = less than 10% total cost 1.5 = 10%–30% total cost 2 = 30%–60% total cost 3 = greater than 60% of total cost

"Hidden factory costs" is a term used in the lean manufacturing vernacular to refer to expenses that are usually not analyzed or part of metrics but cost companies a large percentage of their business expenses. For example, freight, shipping, and inventory turns are not common metrics that are part of the normal operations/business metrics. In a majority of companies, supply chain is only measured on purchase price variance (PPV), which is the difference between the amount paid per unit and the budgeted amount. This drives behavior to buy large quantities for lower piece part rates at the expense of potential quality issues and holding large quantities of inventory. There are studies that show the true cost of carrying inventory is 10%–15% in addition to the actual cost, and 20%–30% for completed subassemblies and finished product (Trujillo 2013; Hou 2013). If you can't convert inventory to sellable goods quickly, you are holding excess inventory, which can be an issue.

Please note that there are exceptions to all these rules. For example, to get the consistent quality of specific melt of a specific metal alloy, you may have to buy a year's worth of inventory in order to get the mill to produce it. However, these exceptions should be understood, and you will expect these outliers to be recognized during the analysis.

To help further explain this concept, we will use three machine shop suppliers that provide your company similar complex components:

- Supplier A has the best pricing, but quality is only 95%. The PPV looks good because the price is low. It accepts only large orders and your company pays for the freight. It is shipped in a container from overseas and has to clear customs at a high-traffic port, which takes a long time, so large quantities have to be ordered based on the replenishment time (when you go back to the database that you put together, you find that the manufacturing site is in China). Therefore, you are carrying a great deal of its components, and the actual usage has enough inventory for three months.
- Supplier B has great pricing, but quality is only 95%. Its delivery is only 90% because it uses trucking companies that are inconsistent, so you have agreed to pay for the transportation costs. Though the quantity is smaller than a freight container, you don't want to pay for multiple trucks, so the order quantity is roughly two months' worth of production.
- Supplier C's pricing is not as good as the other suppliers, though its quality is 99%. Its delivery performances is very good (99%) because it has implemented kanban/just-in-time (JIT) production methods. However, since it is shipping in only weekly production lot sizes, its inventory turns are much higher. Since this size can be shipped on truck through FedEx or UPS, your company saves on shipping costs.

When you put these factors into the TCO model, you can see that supplier C has the lowest TCO factor of the three suppliers in Table 7.2:

$$\text{TCO} = \text{Quality*Delivery*Inventory*Freight}$$

This means that the cost to buy components from supplier A is over three times the cost of buying components from supplier C based on the TCO factor. Supplier C is half the cost of supplier B.

Major takeaways from this analysis are as follows:

- When you use the TCO model, you can really see how much it's costing you to buy from a supplier using more factors than just quality and delivery.
- You have to use the right metrics to gauge performance, such as inventory turns, since PPV will create results that will lower only the piece part rate while potentially inflating your "hidden factory costs."
- You can use more than these four factors or use your own factors for the analysis. However, be consistent to make sure the analysis is giving you the right information. For example, the percentage of total business you represent at each supplier may be a better indicator than another factor in these calculations.

Table 7.2 Summary of TCO analysis.

		Quality	Delivery	Inventory	Freight
Supplier	TCO	A_1	A_2	A_3	A_4
A	4.20	1.05	1.00	2.00	2.00
B	2.60	1.05	1.10	1.50	1.50
C	1.28	1.01	1.01	1.00	1.25

SUPPLIER CONSOLIDATION: WHAT OTHER FACTORS DRIVE THIS DECISION?

Ending the supplier relationship was probably not on your mind when you first onboarded a new supplier. However, it is something that needs to be thought of, and you need to have an exit strategy that prevents you from compromising product quality and potentially causing risk to patients.

The top reasons for terminating the relationship with a supplier are as follows:

- Consolidation of suppliers for business reasons
- The need for their service has ended
- Poor performance
- Unwilling to comply with repeated requests (e.g., won't document process)
- Unwilling to adapt to the changing environment (e.g., won't accept unannounced audits by registrar if your product contains a CE mark)

The first couple of bullet points have been discussed, and the following paragraphs will discuss the remaining bullets.

As part of your business agreement you should have a clause that allows you to terminate your relationship without paying a gross fee if there is a breach of contract. Part of the breach of contract should include the supplier's performance, unwillingness to comply with repeated requests, and unwillingness to adapt to the changing environment. Part of your exit strategy should include product inventory to cover the onboarding process of a new supplier. It's something that needs to be thought about and included in the business agreement on how to terminate a supplier relationship. The business agreement should cover both your termination of the supplier and your supplier's termination of you as a customer.

Unfortunately, until you start doing business on a daily basis with the supplier, you're not quite sure how it will perform. One of the primary reasons for terminating a supplier relationship is lack of good performance. Your supplier may be continually providing product that does not meet your specifications, but because you are on a tight schedule, you are using this product "as is" or are reworking/repairing the product to meet your specifications. You have spent endless hours trying to work with the supplier to improve its performance, but it continues to provide you product that does not meet your specifications.

In addition to poor performance, your supplier may be unwilling to comply with your repeated requests. Maybe you've sent supplier corrective actions that it refuses to respond to, or maybe it refuses to correct issues that you have raised. It may be unwilling to document its process or to actively show an improvement in overall performance.

Another reason you may terminate the supplier relationship is because the supplier is unwilling to adapt to the changing environment. Living in an FDA- and ISO-regulated industry, we are constantly adapting to regulations. Sometimes these regulations are not driven by the FDA but by environmental concerns. In any case, you will need to adapt to them and your suppliers will need to be active partners in making this happen.

SUPPLIER CONSOLIDATION: EXIT PLAN

The exit plan is just as critical as the original selection and approval steps. For companies that have never gone through a supplier consolidation effort before, we recommend you start with a small pilot program first. After you've completed the pilot program, you'll have a better appreciation for the true amount of effort you'll need to plan.

Starting with a pilot program cannot be stressed enough for any company that has not gone through these efforts before, due to the amount of activities that must be done to perform this as smoothly as possible. No amount of checklists will prepare a company for the true amount of work that is involved until it's done it once. Jim can recall a large company that had attempted to consolidate a large volume of suppliers and create several cross-functional checklists and a very aggressive schedule without piloting out the program. Not only did this include suppliers but multiple manufacturing sites. After nine months of frustration, the program managers admitted that they had taken on too much and the checklists actually prevented them from accomplishing the tasks on the time line. At this point, the management of the company had no choice but to add additional resources to attempt to recover, but the time it took to find and train those people did not help the time line. The company realized that it had to stop the program and reset the time line and deliverables. It took another six months for the company to get back on schedule, and it ended up negatively impacting several customers.

To quote Dwight D. Eisenhower, the 34th president of the United States and supreme commander of the Allied Forces during WWII, "Plans are nothing; planning is everything."

There are many deliverables that should be part of this planning effort, so we have provided a framework for your consideration. The purpose is to add items that are specific to your company and product and remove those that are not.

Phase I—Planning

- Create high-level plan and time line
  - Identify any critical or completion dates that may be important
  - Identify the company's experience and ability to take on the size of this project
- Implement a small pilot program first to see what will work best for your company and your suppliers
- Identify potential suppliers that will support the pilot program
- Create a list of suppliers that will not be part of your future plans
  - Identify the items to transfer
  - Identify any risk or regulatory issues and create the mitigation plan
  - Determine if this transition will be parallel with manufacturing or a transition point
  - If necessary, start the conversation with your impacted customers and/or regulators
  - Document the decisions and put together the master project plan
- Create the team and master project plan
  - Identify which items are being transferred
  - Identify the risk level associated with each item and determine what level of verification or validation is appropriate
- Include the criteria for success
- Identify the implementation plan as well as the post-surveillance plan if appropriate
  - Review the quality performance of the item to identify any other areas that should be reviewed with the new supplier
  - Review the current specifications, drawings, or any associated documents provided to the supplier to ensure they are complete and current

Phase II—Communication

- Project management
  - Identify key people to support the team as well as a project lead and senior sponsor

- Key people represent their function and are responsible for getting feedback on progress (good and bad)
- The managers should agree to free up their daily activities in order to support the effort needed for this project to be successful
  - Communicate decisions and time lines to the team and keep senior sponsor updated
  - Once the objectives are completed, acknowledge the team and close out the team charter
- Identify the suppliers you want to deactivate to future needs
  - Communicate reasons for this change
- Identify the future partners
  - Start the conversation regarding these changes
  - Identify the items and put together a transition plan that is obtainable and meets the business needs
  - Make sure future partners agree with the plan
  - Update all supplier quality–related documents such as the SQA and purchase orders
- Communication plan
  - Discuss strategy plan with customers, suppliers, and regulators at the appropriate time
  - Once decisions are made, overcommunicate the objectives and decisions
  - In your business dealings, treat people with respect ("small world, small industry")
  - Keep internal feedback and communication paths active and open

Phase III—Actions

- Execute activities determined by project deliverables
- Communication plan
  - Create simple dashboards to report status easily
  - Create escalation paths if required
  - Create a log to capture key decisions so these points don't have to be revisited
  - Communicate decisions and time lines to the team and keep senior sponsor updated

Phase IV—Closure

- Communication plan
  - Once the objectives are completed, acknowledge the team and close out the team charter
  - Acknowledge progress when appropriate
  - Conduct lessons learned to determine areas of success and improvement; incorporate those changes into any existing program and procedures for future use

DEACTIVATING AND REACTIVATING SUPPLIERS

As we outlined in the beginning of this chapter, you may have identified some suppliers with which you don't need to have an ongoing business relationship. The only time you may need them is for the annual purchase order from a customer for a special construction that requires this supplier's service. For example, friction welding or soldering or wire crimping may not be part of your normal internal or outsourcing process, but for these annual orders you may need these suppliers.

It makes sense to approach these relationships differently than the machine shop that does only 5% of the entire outsourcing budget, and those items don't represent any significant processes that can't be done by someone else (e.g., CNC machining, Swiss turning).

Here are the six steps to create a deactivating/reactivating process:

1. Identify suppliers
2. Create definition of deactivation
3. Change status to "deactivated"
4. Create process to activate the supplier
5. Create process for situations that are outside process (e.g., time)
6. Monitor

Identify Suppliers

If you were following the consolidation process, you most likely identified the suppliers already. If not, sort your suppliers by annual spend for the last year and you may be able to identify them. More times than not, your supply chain or purchasing lead already knows them by name.

Create Definition of Deactivation

Creating a definition of deactivation should be kept as simple as possible to avoid any confusion. For example, deactivated status means that this supplier has been previously approved, but at this time is not considered for immediate use. This supplier is not considered to be part of the normal purchasing process and is used only in special cases or processes. In this case, the supplier does not require any special reporting or monitoring such as a supplier scorecard. The decision to give this supplier this status is jointly agreed upon by quality and purchasing. This example provides a definition, what is involved, and who can give the supplier this status.

Change Status to "Deactivated"

Now, change the status of these suppliers to "deactivated." Document the change and file the record in the supplier file.

Create Process to Activate the Supplier

Eventually, the time comes that you need to bring this supplier back onto the active list. The steps to do so should be simple and straightforward.

If the supplier has been deactivated for less than a year, then the purchasing lead should contact the supplier to determine whether any changes have occurred with the company, business situation, or quality status. This could be done through an e-mail so the record showing the questions and answers is documented. If no major concerns are identified, then the supplier status is changed from "deactivated" to "active" on the ASL.

Create Process for Situations That Are Outside Process

If the supplier has been deactivated for more than a year, then the purchasing lead should contact the supplier and ask it to provide an updated survey and to identify any significant changes to its business and/or quality status (e.g., ISO certification). The information should be reviewed with the quality lead and a decision should easily be made—approved or not approved.

If the decision is not to approve this supplier for either of these two cases, then a risk assessment should be created to determine the mitigation strategy. For example, if the supplier's ISO certification was removed last year due to poor performance, this will be a different mitigation action. It may require an on-site visit to determine the impact and risk. Once a decision is made, the records should be documented and put in the supplier's file.

Monitor

Before we get to try new processes, there are the groups of people who will bring up the outlier situations that are just not possible to determine at this point. This is common for people who are "risk adverse" and not true change agents. The best way to address this is to create a pilot procedure that allows the process to be monitored for a period of time and for decisions to be made as the situations are identified. No process is perfect when it's first started, since there are normal variations that cannot always be controlled. In this case it's the people and the suppliers, so the best way to address this is to be proactive and keep monitoring the procedure during the initial launch and for the first six months.

SUMMARY/TAKEAWAY

- The project to determine consolidation of suppliers for business or performance reasons needs to be an effectively managed program. If it is done correctly, all parties benefit from the results.
- The TCO model has been shown to be an effective tool to provide an objective analysis of suppliers.
- The consolidation plan is only as good as the implementation plan. You have to dedicate people to the project, not only to create the plan but to implement it.
- Keep your process to deactivate and reactivate suppliers as simple as you can, and monitor it to make sure it works for your company.

Summary of the Book

Here are the takeaways from each chapter.

CHAPTER 1—PURCHASING REGULATIONS

- Warning letters may and in fact do reflect purchasing control issues.
- Use the data to perform a gap assessment of your existing processes. The outcome can not only show areas that need to be addressed but provide a concise report outlining your process that can be shown to external parties.
- Purchasing controls is not "one size fits all"; it needs to be balanced based on the risk of your products and the controls you put in place based on the evaluation of your suppliers. Only you can determine that level.
- Don't create procedures that don't allow for various situations that you will encounter. However, there are some basic elements that have to be covered.

CHAPTER 2—PLANNING

- Start the planning stage of supplier selection with a project charter that includes quality requirements. This is the "GPS" of the project and will help you navigate the process and identify changes to the scope.
- Bring individuals on the team as you need them, and ask them to attend meetings as needed. Be cognizant of their time.
- Use the commodity type to determine what controls are needed based on risk mitigation. The same intensity of evaluation should not be applied to a contract manufacturer of a complex system as that applied to the supplier of a manufacturing aid.
- Apply supplier controls appropriately based on the outcome of the supplier evaluation and the risk profile.

CHAPTER 3—SELECTION OF SUPPLIERS

- The work conducted during planning and selection can be a feeder into the TRF assessment. These activities are building blocks to the next process step, which should not be skipped.

- Remember, "plagiarism is the best form of flattery, but poor implementation of a good idea is just plain bad." So, before you make these steps mandatory within your quality system, perform a pilot test to work out the bugs.
- Onboarding suppliers is just like bringing new employees into the company. Make sure you are ready to spend the appropriate amount of time to help them be successful right from the beginning.
- Have your PCP ready and explain the "mission critical" items.

CHAPTER 4—EVALUATION OF SUPPLIERS

- The evaluation work done in the previous chapters allows the evaluation of the suppliers to be conducted with flexibility and with data that will allow the best decision to be made. Using the TRF tool, the evaluation can be weighted to make sure the more important elements are identified.
- The TRF tool not only allows you to evaluate suppliers against the requirements but highlights the more weighted elements. When comparing suppliers we saw how invaluable that additional information was to make the best decisions.
- The TRF analysis can be documented and is easily defendable in front of any external agency or customer.
- The ASL can be created and maintained in many different ways, but you should pick the method that can be best sustained by your organization.

CHAPTER 5—PROCESS CONTROLS

- Following the steps outlined in this chapter, you can design and implement effective controls that make logistical sense and are robust. The process control plan becomes the record of the work and can be updated as needed.
- Implementing controls at your facility through receiving inspection activities can be done in different ways, from incoming inspection to process control plans and process audits.
- The measurement of the controls can be determined through the cost of quality model.
- Creating the strategic supplier map will help with making a decision on risk mitigation and the intent of pushing the right controls to the closest point possible—at the supplier.
- Communication with your suppliers is critical throughout the relationship.

CHAPTER 6—QUALITY AGREEMENTS

- Review of warning letters reveals the FDA is putting much more scrutiny on SQAs; depending on the risk associated with the product or service, the FDA is looking for much more detailed quality agreements.
- Start with an SQA template and write the agreement commensurate with the risk of the product. Not all suppliers will need a detailed SQA, but all suppliers should receive a change notice form to provide to you for changes to their product or service.
- The SQA should define critical up-front expectations of the supplier and the manufacturer, and these should be maintained throughout the life cycle of the product or service to ensure customers' expectations are met and in some cases regulatory obligations are addressed.

- For suppliers registered with the FDA, the SQA does not replace the supplier's regulatory obligations to be compliant with the FDA's QSReg. It should be a supplement to the supplier's QMS to help define the responsibilities between the finished device manufacturer and the supplier (contract manufacturer).
- When possible, have comparable individuals at each company review and approve the SQA.
- Remember to have an agreement in place that covers the elements of 801.150(e) when shipping product that is to be sterilized to and from your sterilizer.
- Finally, the SQA should be periodically reviewed and updated as needed.

CHAPTER 7—CONSOLIDATION OF SUPPLIERS

- The project to determine consolidation of suppliers for business or performance reasons needs to be an effectively managed program. If it is done correctly, all parties benefit from the results.
- The TCO model has been shown to be an effective tool to provide an objective analysis of suppliers.
- The consolidation plan is only as good as the implementation plan. You have to dedicate people to the project, not only to create the plan but to implement it.
- Keep your process to deactivate and reactivate suppliers as simple as you can, and monitor it to make sure it works for your company.

References

ANSI/ASQC Z1.4-2003. *Sampling Procedures and Tables for Inspection by Attributes*. Milwaukee, WI: ASQ Quality Press.

ANSI/ASQ Z1.9-2003 (R2013). 2013. *Sampling Procedures and Tables for Inspection by Variables for Percent Nonconforming*.

Devine, Christopher. 2009. "Exploring the Effectiveness of Defensive-Receiving Inspection for Medical Device Manufacturers: A Mixed Method Study." PhD diss., Northcentral University, Prescott Valley, AZ.

Hou, Billy. 2013. "Do You Know Your Inventory Carrying Costs?" *OPS Rules* (blog), September 10, http://www.opsrules.com/supply-chain-optimization-blog/bid/314279/Do-You-Know-Your-Inventory-Carrying-Costs.

Juran, Joseph M., and A. Blanton Godfrey. 1999. *Juran's Quality Handbook*. 5th ed. New York: McGraw-Hill.

Schmitt, Shawn M. 2008. "Changes May Be In Store for FDA's Quality System Inspection Technique." March 1, "The Silver Sheet." Pharma intelligence Informa. https://www.pharmamedtechbi.com/publications/the-silver-sheet/12/003/changes-may-be-in-store-for-fdas-quality-system-inspection-technique.

Trautman, Kim. 2012. "Supplier Controls: FDA Perspective." MEDCON presentation, Xavier University. http://xavierhealth.org/wp-content/uploads/Trautman_Purchasing-Controls.pdf

Trujillo, Paul. 2013. "The Real Cost of Carrying Inventory." Wasp Buzz, http://www.waspbarcode.com/buzz/real-cost-carrying-inventory/.

US Food and Drug Administration. 2011. *Compliance Program Guidance Manual*. Program 7382.845, Inspection of Medical Device Manufacturers. http://www.fda.gov/downloads/medicaldevices/deviceregulationandguidance/guidancedocuments/ucm244277.pdf.

———. 2015. Investigations Operations Manual. http://www.fda.gov/ICECI/Inspections/IOM/ucm122534.htm.

Index

Note: Page numbers followed by *f* or *t* refer to figures or tables, respectively.

E

F

G

H

I

J

K

L

M

N

O

T

V

W

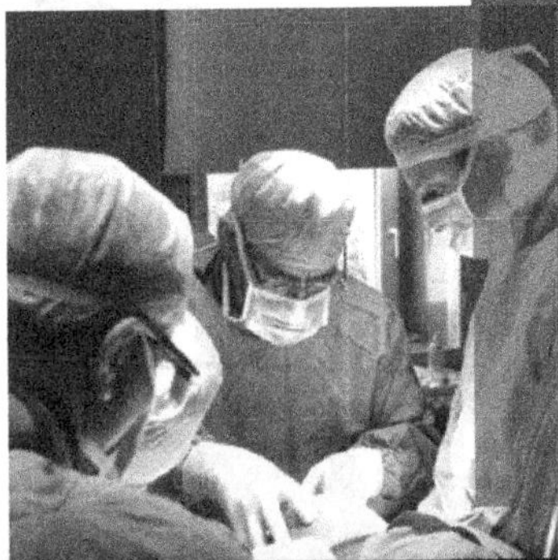